Bibliography of Groundwater Resources of the Glacial-Aquifer Systems in Washington, Idaho, and Northwestern Montana, 1905–2011

By Sue C. Kahle and Zoe O. Futornick

Groundwater Resources Program

Open-File Report 2012–1053

U.S. Department of the Interior
U.S. Geological Survey

U.S. Department of the Interior
KEN SALAZAR, Secretary

U.S. Geological Survey
Marcia K. McNutt, Director

U.S. Geological Survey, Reston, Virginia: 2012

For more information on the USGS—the Federal source for science about the Earth, its natural and living resources, natural hazards, and the environment—visit *http://www.usgs.gov* or call 1–888–ASK–USGS

For an overview of USGS information products, including maps, imagery, and publications, visit *http://www.usgs.gov/pubprod*

To order this and other USGS information products, visit *http://store.usgs.gov*

Suggested citation:
Kahle, S.C. and Futornick, Z.O., 2012, Bibliography of groundwater resources of the glacial aquifer systems in Washington, Idaho, and northwestern Montana, 1905–2011: U.S. Geological Survey Open-File Report 2012-1053, 32 p.

Contents

Figure

Bibliography of Groundwater Resources of the Glacial-Aquifer Systems in Washington, Idaho, and Northwestern Montana, 1905–2011

By Sue C. Kahle and Zoe O. Futornick

Abstract

The U.S. Geological Survey Groundwater Resources Program is undertaking a series of regional groundwater availability studies to improve our understanding of groundwater availability in major aquifers across the Nation. One of the objectives of the Glacial Principal Aquifers study (proposed) is to provide information on the occurrence of groundwater in glacial aquifers in the United States, an area that includes parts of the northern continental States and much of Alaska. Toward this effort, a literature search was conducted to identify readily available documents that describe the occurrence of groundwater in glacial aquifers in the United States. This bibliography provides citations for documents, as well as codes indicating types of information available in each, for Washington, Idaho, and northwestern Montana—an area corresponding approximately to the southern extent of the Cordilleran ice sheet.

Introduction

Groundwater is among the Nation's most important natural resources. Groundwater provides one-half of the Nation's drinking water and is essential to the vitality of agriculture and industry, as well as to the health of rivers, wetlands, and estuaries throughout the Nation. Large-scale development of groundwater resources with accompanying declines in groundwater levels and other effects of pumping has led to concerns about the future availability of groundwater to meet domestic, agricultural, industrial, and environmental needs. The U.S. Geological Survey (USGS) Groundwater Resources Program (GWRP) is undertaking a series of regional groundwater availability studies to improve our understanding of groundwater availability in major aquifers across the Nation.

Information on the glacial-aquifer systems in Washington, Idaho, and Montana is found in many reports and printed and computerized bibliographies and indexes. This report compiles this information into one document—an inclusive bibliography about groundwater resources of glacial-aquifer systems in Washington, Idaho, and northwestern Montana.

Purpose and Scope

The purpose of this bibliography is to provide a list of published literature relating to groundwater resources of the glacial aquifer systems in Washington, Idaho, and northwestern Montana, corresponding to an area within or near the southern extent of the Cordilleran Ice Sheet within the continental United States (fig. 1).

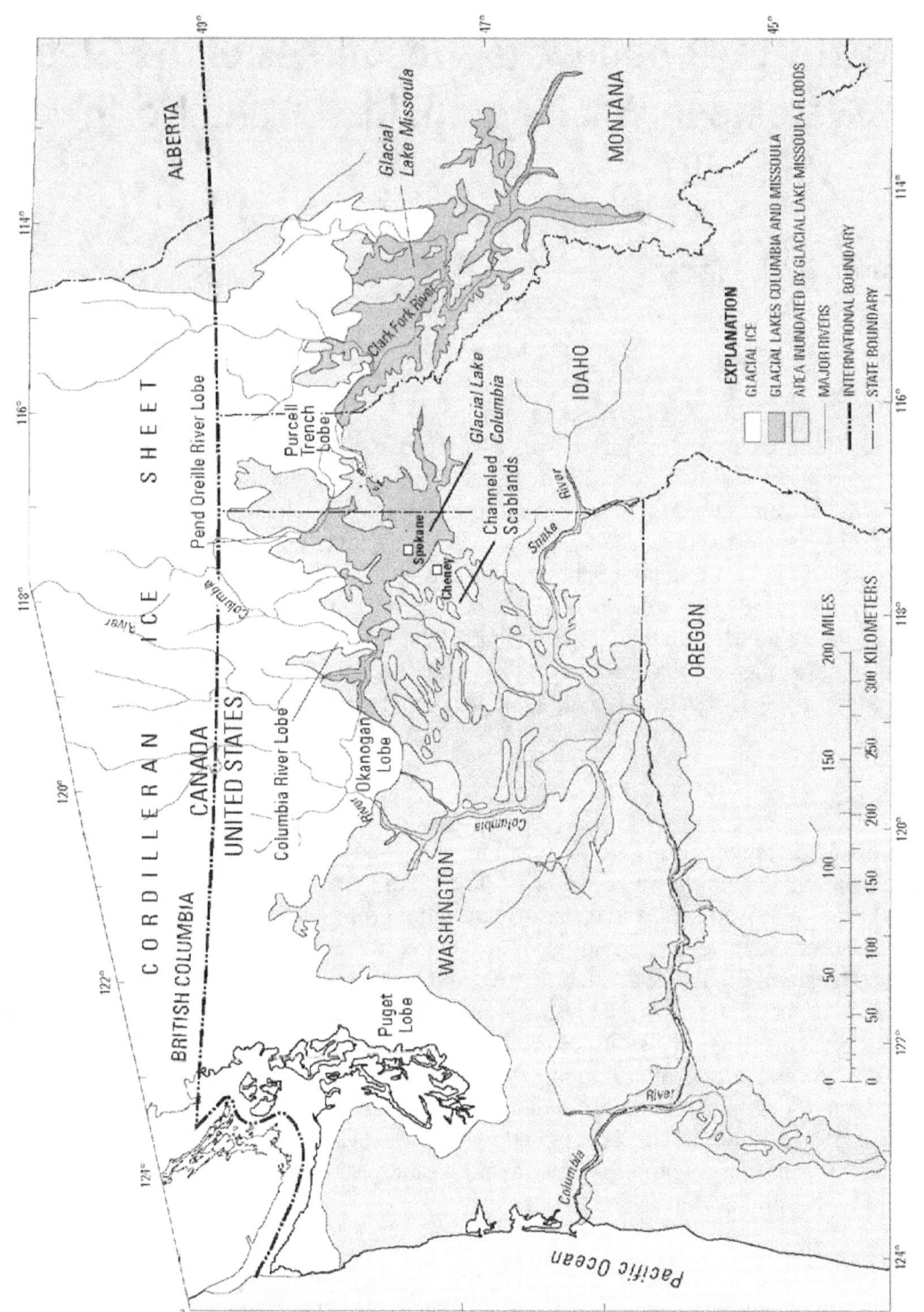

Figure 1. Extent of the Cordilleran Ice Sheet in Washington, Idaho, and northwestern Montana.

2

References contained in this bibliography date from 1905 through 2011. The focus of this bibliography is to include references that describe the physical nature of groundwater systems. In the interest of providing a manageable bibliography focused on groundwater systems, documents pertaining only to water chemistry, surface water, or geology generally were not included. The bibliography contains references to government and other technical reports, selected theses, maps, journal articles, books, and several fact sheets. Most documents in this bibliography are for regional areas of study. For some areas, small-scale studies are included if regional studies have not been conducted. Unpublished documents, publications in press, conference abstracts, and site-specific (small-scale) geotechnical reports generally are omitted from the bibliography.

Approach

This bibliography was compiled from numerous USGS and State resources. In addition to author publications lists, various published atlases and bibliographies were used to identify documents to include in this bibliography including Briar and others (1996), Clark and Dutton (1996), Jones (1990), MacInnis and others (2009), Tuck and others (1996), and Whitehead (1994, 1996). Additional documents were identified in on-line publication lists and bibliographies hosted by the USGS Water Science Centers in Washington (*http://wa.water.usgs.gov/pubs/*), Idaho (*http://id.water.usgs.gov/publications/*), and Montana (*http://mt.water.usgs.gov/pub/Biblio.html*).

State resources include on-line bibliographies and publication lists hosted by the:
- Washington Department of Ecology (*http://www.ecy.wa.gov/biblio/groundwater.html* and *http://www.ecy.wa.gov/programs/eap/wsb/wsb_Geology-and-Groundwater.html*);
- Washington Division of Geology and Earth Resources (*http://www.dnr.wa.gov/ResearchScience/Topics/GeologyPublicationsLibrary/Pages/washbib.aspx*), the Idaho Department of Water Resources, (*http://www.idwr.idaho.gov/WaterInformation/Publications/* and *http://www.idwr.idaho.gov/WaterInformation/Projects/svrp*),
- Idaho Geological Survey (igs@uidaho.edu), and
- Montana Bureau of Mines and Geology (*http://www.mbmg.mtech.edu/mbmgcat/catMain.asp*).

The bibliography is arranged by State and alphabetically by principal author (individual or organization): where more than one publication by the same author is listed, the references are in chronological order. A "Regional Studies" section includes references to reports that discuss the groundwater of broad regional or large, multistate areas such as the Spokane Valley–Rathdrum Prairie aquifer, which covers parts of Washington and Idaho.

To supplement the bibliography, each reference is assigned codes that identify principal types of information it contains (Wiltshire, and others, 1986). These codes, given at the end of each reference, are defined as:

B   Hydrologic budget of aquifers or aquifer systems, or components thereof, such as 'recharge'
C   Water-chemistry data in tables and/or maps
D   Geologic and well data in tables and/or maps
G   Geologic description of aquifers (or hydrogeologic units)
H   Hydrologic description of groundwater systems
K   Hydraulic properties of geologic materials
L   Water-level data in tables and/or maps
M   Mathematical model of groundwater systems
Q   Analysis of groundwater-quality data
R   Reconnaissance appraisal of aquifers, usually presented as maps
S   Description of surface-water resources
U   Water-use data or summary of water use for a locality

Documents listed in **bold type** were not readily available for review at the time of publication (2012) and, therefore, do not have codes assigned indicating the type of information contained in the document.

Bibliography of Groundwater Resources of the Glacial-Aquifer Systems

Regional Studies

Citation	Information codes
Anderson, K.E., 1951, Geology and ground-water resources of the Rathdrum Prairie project and contiguous area, Idaho-Washington: Bureau of Reclamation, Kalispell Planning Office, 39 p., 3 pls.	C,D,G,L,Q
Bartolino, J.R., 2007, Assessment of areal recharge to the Spokane Valley-Rathdrum Prairie aquifer, Spokane County, Washington, and Bonner and Kootenai Counties, Idaho: U.S. Geological Survey Scientific Investigations Report 2007-5038, 38 p. (Available at http://pubs.er.usgs.gov/publication/sir20075038.)	B
Berenbrock, Charles, Bassick, M.D., Rogers, T.L., and Garcia, S.P., 1995, Depth to water, 1991, in the Rathdrum Prairie, Idaho; Spokane River valley, Washington; Moscow-Lewiston-Grangeville area, Idaho; and selected intermontane valleys, east-central Idaho: U.S. Geological Survey Water-Resources Investigations Report 94-4087, 2 sheets. (Available at *http://pubs.er.usgs.gov/publication/wri944087.*)	L

Bolke, E.L., and Vaccaro, J.J., 1981, Digital-model simulation of the hydrologic flow system, with emphasis on ground water in the Spokane Valley, Washington and Idaho: U.S. Geological Survey Open-File Report 80–1300, 43 p. (Available at *http://pubs.er.usgs.gov/publication/ofr801300;* document accessed March 8, 2012, at *http://www.deq.idaho.gov/media/528122-h6.pdf.*)   B,G,H,K,M

Bortleson, G.C., and Ebbert, J.C., 2000, Occurrence of pesticides in streams and ground water in the Puget Sound basin, Washington, and British Columbia, 1996–98: U.S. Geological Survey Water-Resources Investigations Report 00-4118, 14 p. (Available at *http://pubs.er.usgs.gov/publication/wri004148.*)   C,Q

Bowers, C.L., Caldwell, R.R., and Dutton, D.M., 2003, Water-quality, streambed-sediment, and biological data from the Clark Fork-Pend Oreille and Spokane River basins, Montana, Idaho, and Washington, 1998–2001: U.S. Geological Survey Open-File Report 03-292, 203 p. (Available at *http://pubs.er.usgs.gov/publication/ofr03292.*)   C,L,Q

Briar, D.W., Lawlor, S.M., Stone, M.A.J., Parliman, D.J., Schaefer, J.L., and Kendy, Eloise, 1996, Ground-water levels in the intermontane basins of the northern Rocky Mountains, Montana and Idaho: U.S. Geological Survey Hydrologic Investigations Atlas HA-738-B, 1 sheet, scale 1:750,000. (Available at *http://pubs.er.usgs.gov/publication/ha738B.*)   L

Buchanan, J.P., 2000, Unified groundwater flow model of the Rathdrum Prairie-Spokane Valley aquifer system: Prepared for Water Quality Management Program, Spokane County Public Works and Idaho Division of Environmental Quality: Cheney, Eastern Washington University, 23 p. (accessed March 8, 2012, at *http://www.deq.idaho.gov/media/528186-h1.pdf*).   H,K,M

Caldwell, R.R., Bowers, C.L., and Dutton, D.M., 2004, Ground-water quality of selected basin-fill aquifers of the northern Rockies intermontane basins in Montana, Idaho, and Washington: U.S. Geological Survey Scientific Investigations Report 2004-5052, 50 p. (Available at *http://pubs.er.usgs.gov/publication/sir20045052.*)   C,D,G,H, K,Q

Caldwell, R.R., and Bowers, C.L., 2003, Surface-water/ground-water interaction of the Spokane River and the Spokane Valley/Rathdrum Prairie aquifer, Idaho and Washington: U.S. Geological Survey Water-Resources Investigations Report 03–4239, 60 p. (Available at *http://pubs.er.usgs.gov/publication/wri034239.*)   C,D,G,H, K,Q,U

Campbell, A.M., 2005, Ground-water levels in the Spokane Valley–Rathdrum Prairie aquifer, Spokane County, Washington, and Bonner and Kootenai Counties, Idaho, September 2004: U.S. Geological Survey Scientific Investigations Map 2905, 1 sheet. (Available at *http://pubs.er.usgs.gov/publication/sim2905.*)   D,H,L

Clark, G.M., Caldwell, R.R., Maret, T.R., Bowers, C.L., Dutton, D.M., and Beckwith, M.A., 2004, Water quality in the Northern Rockies Intermontane Basins, Idaho, Montana, and Washington, 1999–2001: U.S. Geological Survey Circular 1235, 35 p. (Available at *http://pubs.er.usgs.gov/publication/cir1235.*)   Q,U

Clark, G.M., Maret, T.R., Rupert, M.G., Maupin, M.A., Low, W.H., and Ott, D.S., 1998, Water quality in the upper Snake River Basin, Idaho and Wyoming, 1992–95: U.S. Geological Survey Circular 1160, 35 p. (Available at *http://pubs.er.usgs.gov/publication/cir1160.*)   C,Q,S,U

Clark, D.W., and Dutton, D.M., 1996, Quality of ground water and surface water in intermontane basins of the northern Rocky Mountains, Montana and Idaho: U.S. Geological Survey Hydrologic Investigations Atlas HA-738-C, 1 sheet, scale 1:750,000. (Available at *http://pubs.er.usgs.gov/publication/ha738.*) — C,Q

Clark, D.W., and Kendy, Eloise, 1992, Plan of study for the Regional Aquifer-System Analysis of the Northern Rocky Mountains Intermontane Basins, Montana and Idaho: U.S. Geological Survey Water-Resources Investigations Report 92-4116, 16 p. (Available at *http://pubs.er.usgs.gov/publication/wri924116.*) — G,H,K

Cox, S.E., and Kahle, S.C., 1999, Hydrogeology, ground-water quality, and sources of nitrate in lowland glacial aquifers of Whatcom County, Washington, and British Columbia, Canada: U.S. Geological Survey Water-Resources Investigations Report 98-4195, 251 p. (Available at *http://pubs.er.usgs.gov/publication/wri984195.*) — B,C,D,G, H,K,L,Q

Cox, S.E., and Liebscher, Hugh, 1999, Ground-water quality data from the Abbotsford-Sumas aquifer of southwestern British Columbia and northwestern Washington State, February 1997: U.S. Geological Survey Open-File Report 99-244, 28 p. (Available at *http://pubs.er.usgs.gov/publication/ofr99244.*) — C,D,H,L,Q

Drost, B.W., and Seitz, H.R., 1978, Spokane Valley–Rathdrum Prairie aquifer, Washington and Idaho: U.S. Geological Survey Open-File Report 77-829, 78 p. (Available at *http://pubs.er.usgs.gov/publication/ofr77829.*) — C,D,G,H,K, Q,S,U

Fosdick, E.R., 1931, A study of ground water in the Spokane and Rathdrum Valleys: The Washington Water Power Company, 34 p., 8 pls. (Available at Washington State University Library Special Collections.) — R

Foxworthy B.L., 1979, Summary appraisals of the nation's ground-water resources, Pacific Northwest Region: U.S. Geological Survey Professional Paper 813-S, 39 p. (Available at *http://pubs.er.usgs.gov/publication/pp813S.*) — B,D,G,H, Q,U

Gearhart, C.M., 2001, The hydraulic connection between the Spokane River and the Spokane Aquifer—Gaining and losing reaches of the Spokane River from state line, Idaho to Spokane, Washington: Cheney, Eastern Washington University, M.S. thesis, 106 p. — H,S

Halstead, E.C., 1986, Ground water supply–Fraser lowland, British Columbia: Environment Canada, National Hydrology Research Institute Paper no. 26, Inland Waters Directorate Scientific Series no. 145, 80 p. — C,D,G, H,L,Q

Hortness, J.E., and Covert, J.J., 2005, Streamflow trends in the Spokane River and tributaries, Spokane Valley/Rathdrum Prairie, Idaho and Washington: U.S. Geological Survey Scientific Investigations Report 2005-5005, 18 p. (Available at *http://pubs.er.usgs.gov/publication/sir20055005.*) — S

Hsieh, P.A., Barber, M.E., Contor, B.A., Hossain, Md.A., Johnson, G.S., Jones, J.L., and Wylie, A.H., 2007, Ground-water flow model for the Spokane Valley-Rathdrum Prairie Aquifer, Spokane County, Washington, and Bonner and Kootenai Counties, Idaho: U.S. Geological Survey Scientific Investigations Report 2007-5044, 78 p. (Available at *http://pubs.er.usgs.gov/publication/sir20075044.*) — B,D,G,H, K,L,M,S,U

Inkpen, E.L., Tesoriero, A.J., Ebbert, J.C., Silva, S.R., and Sandstrom, M.W., 2000, Ground-water quality in regional, agricultural, and urban settings in the Puget Sound Basin, Washington and British Columbia, 1996–1998: U.S. Geological Survey Water-Resources Investigations Report 00-4100, 66 p. (Available at *http://pubs.er.usgs.gov/publication/wri004100*.)   C,Q,U

Jones, M.A., 1999, Geologic framework of the Puget Sound aquifer system, Washington and British Columbia: U.S. Geological Survey Professional Paper 1424-C, 31 p., 18 pls. (Available at *http://pubs.er.usgs.gov/publication/pp1424C*.)   D,G,H

Jones, M.A., 1996, Thickness of unconsolidated deposits in the Puget Sound lowland, Washington and British Columbia: U.S. Geological Survey Water-Resources Investigations Report 94-4133, 1 pl., scale 1:500,000. (Available at *http://pubs.er.usgs.gov/publication/wri944133*.)   D,G

Kahle, S.C., and Bartolino, J.R., 2007, Hydrogeologic framework and ground-water budget of the Spokane Valley-Rathdrum Prairie Aquifer, Spokane County, Washington, and Bonner and Kootenai Counties, Idaho: U.S. Geological Survey Scientific Investigations Report 2007-5041, 48 p. (Available at *http://pubs.er.usgs.gov/publication/sir20075041*.)   B,D,G,H, K,S,U

Kahle, S.C., Caldwell, R.R., and Bartolino, J.R., 2005, Compilation of geologic, hydrologic, and ground-water flow modeling information for the Spokane Valley-Rathdrum Prairie Aquifer, Spokane County, Washington, and Bonner and Kootenai Counties, Idaho: U.S. Geological Survey Scientific Investigations Report 2005-5227, 64 p. (Available at *http://pubs.er.usgs.gov/publication/sir20055227*.)   B,D,G,H, K,L,M,S,U

MacInnis, J.D., Lackaff, B.B., Buchanan, J.P., Boese, R.M., McHugh, J., Harvey, G., Higdem, R., and Stevens, G., 2009, The Spokane Valley-Rathdrum Prairie aquifer atlas 2009 update: Spokane, Spokane Aquifer Joint Board, 26 p. (accessed March 8, 2012, at *http://www.spokanecounty.org/loaddoc.aspx?docid=4487*).   B,D,G,Q,U

Murray, Lindy, 2007, Evaluation of boundary conditions and ground-water/surface-water flux at lakes bordering the Spokane Valley-Rathdrum Prairie aquifer, Washington and Idaho: Idaho Falls, University of Idaho, M.S. thesis.   B,G,L

Oldow, J.S., and Sprenke, K.F., 2006, Gravity acquisition and depth to basement modeling of the Spokane Valley and Rathdrum Prairie Aquifer, northeastern Washington and northwestern Idaho: Moscow, University of Idaho, 15 p. (accessed March 12, at *http://www.idwr.idaho.gov/WaterInformation/projects/svrp/Publications/PDFs/SVRP_Report.pdf*).   G

Piper, A.M., and Huff, L.C., 1943, Some ground-water features of the Rathdrum Prairie-Spokane Valley area, Idaho-Washington, with respect to seepage loss from Pend Oreille Lake: U.S. Geological Survey Report, 13 p., 2 pls.   B,G,S

Piper, A.M., and La Rocque, G.A., Jr., 1944, Water-table fluctuations in the Spokane Valley and contiguous area Washington–Idaho: U.S. Geological Survey Water-Supply Paper 889-B, p. 83-139, 2 pls. (Available at *http://pubs.er.usgs.gov/publication/wsp889B*.)   D,G,H,L,S

Pluhowski, E.J., and Thomas, C.A., 1968, A water-balance equation for the Rathdrum Prairie ground-water reservoir, near Spokane, Washington: U.S. Geological Survey Professional Paper 600-D, p. D75-D78. (Available at *http://pubs.er.usgs.gov/publication/pp600D*.)   B,H

Scibek, Jacek, 2005, Modelling the impacts of climate change on groundwater—A comparative study of two unconfined aquifers in southern British Columbia and northern Washington State: Vancouver, British Columbia, Simon Fraser University, PhD dissertation, 1 v.]   B,H,K,M

Sprenke, K.F., 2006, Evaluation of existing gravity observations in the Rathdrum Spokane Aquifer: Moscow, University of Idaho, Final Report: Contract # CON00693: Technical Assistance for Spokane-Rathdrum Hydrologic Modeling and Studies Project, Idaho Department of Water Resources, 15 p. (accessed March 8, 2012, at *http://www.idwr.idaho.gov/WaterInformation/Projects/svrp/Publications/PDFs/Sprenk eFinalReport.pdf*).   G

Thomas, C.A., 1963, Investigation of the inflow to the Rathdrum Prairie–Spokane Valley aquifer: U.S. Geological Survey Open-File Report 63-121, 46 p., 7 pls. (Available at *http://pubs.er.usgs.gov/publication/ofr62121*.)   B

Tornes, L.H., 1997, National Water-Quality Assessment Program—Northern Rockies Intermontane Basins: U.S. Geological Survey Fact Sheet FS-158-97, 4 p. (Available at *http://pubs.er.usgs.gov/publication/fs1589*.)   C,G,Q,S,U

Tuck, L.K., Briar, D.W., and Clark, D.W., 1996, Geologic history and hydrogeologic units of intermontane basins of the northern Rocky Mountains, Montana and Idaho: U.S. Geological Survey Hydrologic Investigations Atlas HA-738-A, scale 1:750,000, sheet 1. (Available at *http://pubs.er.usgs.gov/publication/ha738A*.)   G

Vaccaro, J.J., 1992, Plan of study for the Puget-Willamette Lowland Regional Aquifer-System analysis, western Washington and western Oregon: U.S. Geological Survey Water-Resources Investigations Report 91-4189, 41 p. (Available at *http://pubs.er.usgs.gov/publication/wri914189*.)   B,G,H,K,M, Q,U

Vaccaro, J.J., and Bolke, E.L., 1983, Evaluation of water-quality characteristic of part of the Spokane aquifer, Washington and Idaho, using a solute-transport model: U.S. Geological Survey Water-Resources Investigations Open-File Report 82-769, 69 p. (Available at *http://pubs.er.usgs.gov/publication/ofr82769*.)   G,H,K,M,Q

Vaccaro, J.J., Hansen, A.J., and Jones, M.A., 1998, Hydrogeologic framework of the Puget Sound aquifer system, Washington and British Columbia: U.S. Geological Survey Professional Paper 1424-D, 77 p. (Available at *http://pubs.er.usgs.gov/publication/pp1424*.)   B,G,H,K, M,Q,U

Vaccaro, J.J., Woodward, D.G., Gannett, M.W., Jones, M.A., Collins, C.A., and Caldwell, R.R., 1997, Summary of the Puget-Willamette Lowland regional aquifer-system analysis, Washington, Oregon, and British Columbia: U.S. Geological Survey Open-File Report 96-353, 49 p. (Available at *http://pubs.er.usgs.gov/publication/ofr96353*.)   B,D,G,H,K, Q,U

Whitehead, R.L., 1996, Ground-water atlas of the United States, segment 8, Montana, North Dakota, South Dakota, and Wyoming: U.S. Geological Survey Hydrologic Investigations Atlas HA-730-I, 24 p. (Available at *http://pubs.er.usgs.gov/publication/ha730I*.)   D,G,H,Q

Whitehead, R.L., 1994, Ground-water atlas of the United States, segment 7, Idaho, Oregon, and Washington: U.S. Geological Survey Hydrologic Investigations Atlas HA-730-H, 31 p. (Available at *http://pubs.er.usgs.gov/publication/ha730H*.)   D,G,H,Q

Idaho

Citation	Information codes
Adema, G.W., 1999, Bedrock depth and morphology of the Rathdrum Prairie, Idaho: Moscow, University of Idaho, M.S. thesis, 67 p.	D,G
Baker, S.J., 1987, Ground-water conditions in the Blanchard-Oldtown area: Idaho Department of Water Resources, 10 p. (accessed March 8, 2012, at *http://www.idwr.idaho.gov/WaterInformation/Publications/ofr/ofr-gw_conditions_blanchard-oldtown.pdf*).	D,L,R
Baldwin, J., and McVay, M., 2008, Ground water report, Silverwood area of the Rathdrum Prairie Sensitive Resource Aquifer: Boise, Idaho Department of Environmental Quality Ground Water Quality Technical Report No. 32, 27 p. (accessed March 8, 2012, at *http://www.deq.idaho.gov/media/470739-_water_data_reports_ground_water_silverwood_32.pdf*).	Q
Baldwin, J., and Owsley, D., 2005, The Ramsey Channel of the Spokane Valley-Rathdrum Prairie Aquifer: Idaho Department of Environmental Quality Technical Ground Water Report No. 26, 23 p. (accessed March 8, 2012, at *http://www.deq.idaho.gov/media/528158-h16.pdf*).	D,G,H,L
Buchanan, J.P., 1989, Reconnaissance hydrogeologic study of the Kootenai River valley near Bonners Ferry, Idaho: Upper Columbia United Tribes Fisheries Center Fisheries Technical Report no. 25, variously paged.	
Burnham, W.L., and others, 1966, Summary of ground-water conditions in Idaho, 1966: Idaho Department of Reclamation Water Information Bulletin 1, 64 p. (accessed March 8, 2012, at *http://www.idwr.idaho.gov/WaterInformation/Publications/wib/wib01-gw_conditions_id.pdf*).	R
Campbell, A.M., 2006, Availability of ground-water data for Idaho, water year 2006: U.S. Geological Survey Fact Sheet 2007-3031, 2 p. (Available at *http://pubs.er.usgs.gov/publication/fs20103113.*)	R
Cisco, H.G., and Whitehead, R.L., 1969, Ground-water levels in Idaho, 1969: Idaho Department of Reclamation Water Information Bulletin No. 11, 75 p. (accessed March 8, 2012, at *http://www.idwr.idaho.gov/WaterInformation/Publications/wib/wib11-gw_levels_id_1969.pdf*).	L
Clarkson, D., and Buchanan, J.P., 1998, A reconnaissance of the hydrogeology and ground water quality in three hillside basins at the perimeter of the Rathdrum Prairie aquifer in Kootenai County, Idaho: Prepared for the Idaho Division of Environmental Quality: Cheney, Eastern Washington University, 103 p. (accessed March 8, 2012, at *http://www.deq.idaho.gov/media/528170-h2.pdf*).	C,D,G,H, L,Q,R

Dion, N.P, and Whitehead, R.L., 1973, A ground-water monitoring network for Kootenai   L,R
    Flats, northern Idaho: Idaho Department of Water Administration Water Information
    Bulletin No. 33, 47 p. (accessed March 8, 2012, at
    http://www.idwr.idaho.gov/WaterInformation/Publications/wib/wib33-
    network_kootenai_flats.pdf).

Fader, S.W., 1951, Water levels in wells and lakes in Rathdrum Prairie and contiguous   D,L
    areas, Bonner and Kootenai Counties, northern Idaho: U.S. Geological Survey Open-
    File Report 51-17, 90 p. (Available at *http://pubs.er.usgs.gov/publication/ofr5117.*)

Graham, W.A., and Buchanan, J.P., 1994, Hydrogeologic characterization and   C,D,G,H,
    reconnaissance water quality study of the Chilco Channel Area, Kootenai County,   L,Q,R
    Idaho: Eastern Washington University, prepared for Idaho Department of
    Environmental Quality, 135 p. (accessed March 8, 2012, at
    http://www.deq.idaho.gov/media/528150-h3.pdf).

Graham, W.G., and Campbell, L.J., 1981, Ground-water resources of Idaho: Idaho   R,U
    Department of Water Resources, 61 p. (accessed March 8, 2012, at
    http://www.idwr.idaho.gov/WaterInformation/Publications/misc/Ground_Water_Resou
    rces_ID.pdf).

Gregory, Guy, and Covert, John, 2006, Spokane River temperature profile, Barker Road   H,S
    to Plantes Ferry Park, September 2005: Olympia, Washington Department of Ecology,
    Publication No. 06-11-005, 23 p. (accessed March 8, 2012, at
    http://www.ecy.wa.gov/biblio/0611005.html).

Hammond, R.E., 1974, Ground-water occurrence and movement in the Athol area and   D,G,R
    the northern Rathdrum Prairie, northern Idaho: Idaho Department of Water
    Administration Water Information Bulletin 35, 19 p., 3 pls. (accessed March 8, 2012,
    at *http://www.idwr.idaho.gov/WaterInformation/Publications/wib/wib35-*
    gw_athol_rathdrum_prairie.pdf).

Hortness, J.E., and Berenbrock, Charles, 2001, Estimating monthly and annual   S
    streamflow statistics at ungaged sites in Idaho: U.S. Geological Survey Water-
    Resources Investigations Report 01-4093, 36 p. (Available at
    http://pubs.er.usgs.gov/publication/wri014093).

Jehn, P., 1988, The Rathdrum Prairie aquifer technical report: Idaho Department of   Q
    Health and Welfare, Division of Environmental Quality, Bureau of Water Quality,
    90 p. (accessed March 8, 2012, at *http://www.deq.idaho.gov/media/473738-rathdrum-*
    prairie-aquifer-entire-0888.pdf).

Jensen, J.R., and Eckart, C.M., 1987, The Spokane aquifer: Washington State   H,R
    Department of Natural Resources, Division of Geology and Earth Resources Bulletin,
    v. 78, no. II, p. 975-981.

Kinnison, P.T., A survey of the ground water of the state of Idaho: Idaho Bureau of   R
    Mines and Geology, 51 p. (accessed March 8, 2012, at
    http://www.idahogeology.org/PDF/Pamphlets_(P)/p-103.pdf).

Lum, W.E., Turney, G.L., and Alvord, R.C., 1986, A preliminary evaluation of the   C,D,G,
    geohydrology and water quality of the Greenacres landfill area, Spokane County,   L,Q
    Washington: U.S. Geological Survey Open-File Report 85-496, 41 p. (Available at
    http://pubs.er.usgs.gov/publication/ofr85496.)

Marti, P.B., and Garrigues, R.S., 2001, Spokane River/aquifer interaction project results,   B,S
May–November 1999: Olympia, Washington State Department of Ecology publication
no. 01-03-024, 40 p.

Maupin, M.A., and Weakland, R.J., 2009, Water budgets for Coeur d'Alene Lake, Idaho,   B
water years 2000–2005: U.S. Geological Survey Scientific Investigations Report 2009-
5184, 16 p. (Available at *http://pubs.er.usgs.gov/publication/sir20095184.*)

Nace, R.L., and Fader, S.W., 1950, Records of wells on Rathdrum Prairie, Bonner and   L
Kootenai Counties, northern Idaho: U.S. Geological Survey Open-File Report 51-19,
50 p., 1 pl. (Available at *http://pubs.er.usgs.gov/publication/ofr5119.*)

Newcomb, R.C., 1975, Groundwater of the Spokane urban area: U.S. Army Corps of   G,H,R
Engineers Water Resources Study, Metropolitan Spokane Region.

Olness, I.A., 1993, Formulation of a finite-difference groundwater flow model for the   M
Spokane Valley aquifer, Washington: Cheney, Eastern Washington University, M.S.
thesis, 101 p.

Packard, F.A., Sumioka, S.S., and Whiteman, K.J., 1983, Ground water-surface water   D,G,H,
relationships in the Bonaparte Creek basin, Okanogan County, Washington, 1979-80:   L,S
U.S. Geological Survey Open-File Report 82-172, 46 p. (Available at
http://pubs.er.usgs.gov/publication/ofr82172.)

Painter, B.D., 1991, An estimate of recharge to the Rathdrum Prairie aquifer in Idaho   B
from all sources: Idaho Department of Health and Welfare, Division of Environmental
Quality, Water Quality Bureau, 6 p.

Palmer, S.P., and Derkey, R.E., 1996, Seismic reflection profiling and well velocity   G
surveying along Colbert Road and Shady Slope Road: Olympia, Washington
Department of Natural Resources, Geology and Earth Resources Division.

Palmer, S.P., and Gerstel, W.J., 1994, Preliminary report on seismic reflection profiling   G
of the Spokane Valley, Spokane County, Washington: Olympia, Washington
Department of Natural Resources, Division of Geology and Earth Resources, 12 p.

Palmer, S.P., King, Michael, Gruenenfelder, C.R., Miller, S.A., and Hendron, L.H.,   G
1995, Application of reflection seismology to the hydrogeology of the Spokane
aquifer: Washington Geology, v. 23, no. 2, p. 27-30.

Parliman, D.J., Seitz, H.R., and Jones, M.L., 1980, Ground-water quality in north Idaho: C,D,G,L,
U.S. Geological Survey Open-File Report 80-596, 34 p. (Available at   Q,R
http://pubs.er.usgs.gov/publication/ofr80596.)

Purves, W.J., 1969, Stratigraphic control of the ground water through Spokane Valley: G,H,K
Pullman, Washington State University, M.S. thesis, 213 p.

Sagstad, S.R., 1977, Hydrogeologic analysis of the southern Rathdrum Prairie area,   C,D,G,H,
Idaho: Moscow, University of Idaho, M.S. thesis, 96 p. (accessed March 8, 2012, at   K,L,Q,R
http://www.deq.idaho.gov/media/528146-h8.pdf).

Seitz, H.R., and Jones, M.L., 1981, Flow characteristics and water-quality conditions in   C,Q,S
the Spokane River, Coeur d'Alene Lake to Post Falls Dam, northern Idaho: U.S.
Geological Survey Open-File Report 82-102, 56 p. (Available at
http://pubs.er.usgs.gov/publication/ofr82102.)

Sisco, H.G., 1974, Ground water levels and well records for current observation wells in   D,L
Idaho, 1922-73: U.S. Geological Survey basic data release, variously paginated.

Spruill, T.B., 1993, Preliminary evaluation of hydrogeology and ground-water quality in valley sediments in the vicinity of Killarney Lake, Kootenai County, Idaho: U.S. Geological Survey Water-Resources Investigations Report 93-4091, 41 p. (Available at *http://pubs.er.usgs.gov/publication/wri934091.*) — H,Q

Stevens, G.R., 2004, Report of geologic/hydrogeologic services Upper Twin Lake Water & Sewer Company, Kootenai County, Idaho: Moscow, Idaho Water Resources Research Institute, University of Idaho, 136 p. — H

Stone, M.A.J., Parliman, D.J., and Schaefer, J.L., 1996, Selected geohydrologic data from a regional aquifer-system analysis of the northern Rocky Mountains intermontane basins in Idaho: U.S. Geological Survey Open-File Report 96-207, 30 p. (Available at *http://pubs.er.usgs.gov/publication/ofr96207.*) — C,D,K,L

U.S. Army Corps of Engineers and Kennedy-Tudor Engineers, 1976, Water resources study metropolitan Spokane region, 13 volumes: Spokane, Wash. — H,Q,S

Walker, E.H., 1964, Ground water in the Sand Point region, Bonner County, Idaho: U.S. Geological Survey Water-Supply Paper 1779-I, 29 p. (Available at *http://pubs.er.usgs.gov/publication/wsp1779I.*) — C,D,G,H, L,Q,R

Whitehead, R.L., and Cisco, H.G., 1968, Ground-water levels in Idaho, 1968: Idaho Department of Reclamation Water Information Bulletin No. 5, 68 p. (accessed March 8, 2012, at *http://www.idwr.idaho.gov/WaterInformation/Publications/wib/wib05-gw_levels_id_1968.pdf*). — L

Wyman, S.A., 1993, The potential for heavy metal migration from sediments of Lake Coeur d'Alene into the Rathdrum Prairie aquifer, Kootenai, Idaho: Moscow, Idaho Water Resources Research Institute, University of Idaho, 158 p. — Q,S

Young, H.W., and Norvitch, R.F., 1984, Ground-water-level trends in Idaho, 1971-82: U.S. Geological Survey Water-Resources Investigations Report 83-4245, 28 p. (Available at *http://pubs.er.usgs.gov/publication/wri834245.*) — L

Northwestern Montana

Citation	Information codes
Abdo, G., 1997, Reappraisal of hydrogeology of the Little Bitteroot Valley, northwestern Montana: Montana Bureau of Mines and Geology, Open-File Report 350, 100 p., 3 sheet(s).	
Alden, W.C., 1953, Physiography and glacial geology of western Montana and adjacent areas: U.S. Geological Survey Professional Paper 231, 200 p. (Available at *http://pubs.er.usgs.gov/publication/pp1231B.*)	D
Boettcher, A.J., 1982, Groundwater resources in the central part of the Flathead Indian Reservation, northwestern Montana: Montana Bureau of Mines and Geology Memoir 48, 28 p.	C,D,G,H, L,Q,S,U
Boettcher, A.J., and Gosling, A.W., 1977, Water resources of the Clark Fork Basin upstream from St. Regis, Montana: Montana Bureau of Mines and Geology Bulletin 104, 28 p.	C,G,H,Q, S,U
Boettcher, A.J., and Wilke, K.R., 1978, Groundwater resources in the Libby Area, northwestern Montana: Montana Bureau of Mines and Geology Bulletin 106, 36 p.	C,D,G,H, L,Q,S
Breitkrietz, Alex, 1966, Basic water data report no. 3, Kalispell Valley, Montana:	D,L

10

Montana Bureau of Mines and Geology Bulletin 53, 25 p.

Breitkrietz, Alex, 1964, Basic water data report no. 1, Missoula Valley, Montana: D,L
Montana Bureau of Mines and Geology Bulletin 37, 43 p.

Briar, D.W., 1987, Water resource analysis of the Sullivan Flats area near Niarada,   C,D,G,H,
Flathead Indian Reservation, Montana: Missoula, University of Montana, M.S. thesis,   K,L,M,Q
184 p.

Cannon, M.R., 1996, Geology and ground-water resources of the Blackfeet Indian   D,G,H,L
Reservation, northwestern Montana: U.S. Geological Survey HA-737. (Available at
http://pubs.er.usgs.gov/publication/ha737.)

Cannon, M.R., and Johnson, D.R., 2004, Estimated water use in Montana in 2000: U.S.   U
Geological Survey Scientific Investigations Report 2004-5223, 50 p. (Available at
http://pubs.er.usgs.gov/publication/sir20045223.)

Carstarphen, C.A., Mason, D.M., Smith, L.N., LaFave, J.I., and Richter, M.G., 2003,   C,D,G,L
Data for water wells visited during the Lolo-Bitterroot Area Ground-Water
Characterization Study—Ravalli, Mineral, and Missoula Counties (open-file version):
Montana Bureau of Mines and Geology, Ground-Water Assessment Atlas 4B-01,
1 sheet(s), 1:250,000 (accessed March 8, 2012, at
http://mbmggwic.mtech.edu/gwcpmaps/gwaa04map01tiled.pdf.)

Chambers, C.L., 1995, Records of wells and water levels for the statewide observation-   D,L
well network in Montana from October 1985 through October 1992: U.S. Geological
Survey Open-File Report 95-432, 153 p. (Available at
http://pubs.er.usgs.gov/publication/ofr95432.)

Clark, D.W., 1994, National Water-Quality Assessment Program—Northern Rockies   R
Intermontane Basins: U.S. Geological Survey Open-File Report 94-124, 2 p.
(Available at *http://pubs.er.usgs.gov/publication/ofr94124.*)

Clark, D.W., and Briar, D.W., 1993, Radon in groundwater of western Montana: U.S.   R
Geological Survey Open-File Report 93-64, 2 p. (Available at
http://pubs.er.usgs.gov/publication/ofr9364.)

Coffin, D.L., Brietkrietz, Alex, and McMurtrey, R.G., 1971, Surficial geology and water   C,D,G,H,
resources of the Tobacco and upper Stillwater River Valleys, northwestern Montana: K,L,Q,S,U
Montana Bureau of Mines and Geology Bulletin 81, 48 p.

Coffin, D.L., and Wilke, K.R., 1971, Water resources of the upper Blackfoot River   C,D,G,H,
Valley, west-central Montana: Montana Department of Natural Resources and   L,Q,R,S
Conservation, Water Resources Division Technical Report Series 1, 82 p.

Davis, R.E., and Rogers, G.D., 1984, Assessment of selected groundwater-quality in   C,Q
Montana: U.S. Geological Survey Water-Resources Investigations Report 84-4173,
177 p. (Available at *http://pubs.er.usgs.gov/publication/wri844173.*)

Donovan, J.J., 1985, Hydrogeologic test data for the Lonepine aquifer, Little
Bitterroot valley, northwestern Montana: Montana Bureau of Mines and
Geology, Open-File Report 162, 10 p.

Donovan, J.J., 1985, Hydrogeology and geothermal resources of the Little Bitterroot   C,D,H,K,
Valley, northwestern Montana: Montana Bureau of Mines and Geology Memoir 58,   L,M,Q
60 p., 2 sheet(s) (accessed March 8, 2012, at *http://www.mbmg.mtech.edu/pdf-
publications/m_58.pdf*).

Dutton, D.M., Lawlor, S.M., Briar, D.W., and Tresch, R.E., 1995, Hydrogeologic data for the northern Rocky Mountains intermontane basins, Montana: U.S. Geological Survey Open-File Report 95-143, 94 p. (Available at *http://pubs.er.usgs.gov/publication/ofr95143.*) — C,D,L

Ferreira, R.F., Cannon, M.R., and Davis, R.E., 1988, Montana groundwater quality, *in* Moody, D.W., Car, Jerry, Chase, E.B., and Paulson, R.W., compilers, National Water Summary 1986—Hydrologic events and groundwater quality: U.S. Geological Survey Water-Supply Paper 2325, p. 339-346. (Available at *http://pubs.er.usgs.gov/publication/wsp2325.*) — Q,R

Johnston, M.F., and Dodge, K.A., 1986, Records of wells and water-level fluctuations from the Statewide Observation-Well Network in Montana through 1985: U.S. Geological Survey Open-File Report 86-528, 221 p. (Available at*http://pubs.er.usgs.gov/publication/ofr86528.*) — D,L

Kendy, Eloise, and Tresch, R.E., 1996, Geographic, geologic, and hydrologic summaries of intermontane basins of the northern Rocky Mountains, Montana: U.S. Geological Survey Water-Resources Investigations Report 96-4025, 233 p. (Available at *http://pubs.er.usgs.gov/publication/wri964025.*) — D,G,H,K, L,R,S

Konizeski, R.L., Brietkrietz, Alex, and McMurtrey, R.G., 1968, Geology and groundwater resources of the Kalispell Valley, northwestern Montana: Montana Bureau of Mines and Geology Bulletin 68, 42 p. (Available at U.S. Geological Survey Menlo Park Library.) — C,D,G,H, K,L,Q

LaFave, J.I., 2006, Potentiometric surface of the basin-fill and bedrock aquifers, Mineral and Missoula Counties, Montana (open-file version), Montana Bureau of Mines and Geology: Ground-Water Assessment Atlas 4B-06, 1 sheet(s), 1:100,000 (accessed March 8, 2012, at *http://mbmggwic.mtech.edu/gwcpmaps/gwaa04map06untiled.pdf*). — L

LaFave, J.I., 2006, Ground-water quality in basin-fill and bedrock aquifers, Mineral and Missoula counties, western Montana (open-file version), Montana Bureau of Mines and Geology: Ground-Water Assessment Atlas 4B-07, 1 sheet(s), 1:500,000 (accessed March 8, 2012, at *http://mbmggwic.mtech.edu/gwcpmaps/gwaa04map07untiled.pdf*). — C,Q

LaFave, J.I., 2006, Potentiometric surface of the shallow basin-fill, deep basin-fill, and bedrock aquifers, Bitterroot Valley, Missoula and Ravalli Counties, western Montana (open-file version), Montana Bureau of Mines and Geology: Ground-Water Assessment Atlas 4B-08, 1 sheet(s), 1:500,000 (accessed March 8, 2012, at *http://mbmggwic.mtech.edu/gwcpmaps/gwaa04map08untiled.pdf*). — L

LaFave, J.I., 2006, Ground-water quality in shallow basin-fill, deep basin-fill, and bedrock aquifers, Bitterroot Valley, Missoula and Ravalli Counties, southwest Montana (open-file version), Montana Bureau of Mines and Geology: Ground-Water Assessment Atlas 4B-09, 1 sheet(s), 1:500,000 (accessed March 8, 2012, at *http://mbmggwic.mtech.edu/gwcpmaps/gwaa04map09untiled.pdf*). — C,Q

LaFave, J.I., 2002, Tracing ground-water flow in the Missoula valley aquifer, southwest Montana, Montana Bureau of Mines and Geology: Ground-Water Open-File Report 17, 16 p. — C,H,Q

LaFave, J.I., 2000, Status of ground-water level monitoring sites, Kalispell Valley (upper Flathead River valley), northwest Montana: Montana Bureau of Mines and Geology, Ground-Water Open-File Report 14, 1 sheet(s), 1:200,000 (accessed March 8, 2012, at *http://mbmggwic.mtech.edu/gwcpmaps/gwof14untiled.pdf*).   L

LaFave, J.I., Smith, L.N., and Patton, T.W., 2004, Ground-water resources of the Flathead Lake Area: Flathead, Lake, and parts of Missoula and Sanders Counties. Part A- Descriptive overview: Montana Bureau of Mines and Geology, Ground-Water Assessment Atlas 2A, 132 p. (accessed March 12, 2012, at *http://www.mbmg.mtech.edu/pdf/GWA_2.pdf*).   C,D,G,H, K,L,Q

Levings, G.W., Ferreira, R.F., and Lambing, J.H., 1984, Water resources of Lake Creek Valley, northwestern Montana: Montana Bureau of Mines and Geology Memoir 56, 81 p.   C,D,G,H, L,Q,S

McDonald, Catherine, and LaFave, J.I., 2004, Groundwater assessment of selected shallow aquifers in the north Flathead Valley and Flathead Lake perimeter, northwest Montana: Montana Bureau of Mines and Geology Open-File Report 492, 40 p.

McMurtrey, R.G., Konizeski, R.L., and Brietkrietz, Alex, 1965, Geology and groundwater resources of the Missoula basin, Montana: Montana Bureau of Mines and Geology Bulletin 47, 35 p.   C,G,H,K, L,Q,R

McMurtrey, R.G., Konizeski, R.L., Stermitz, F., and Swenson, H.A., 1959, Preliminary Report on the Geology and Water Resources of the Bitterroot Valley: Montana Bureau of Mines and Geology Bulletin 9, 45 p.

McMurtrey, R.G., and Reed, T.E., 1968, Water levels and artesian pressures in observation wells in Montana through 1967: Montana Bureau of Mines and Geology Bulletin 65, 40 p.   L

Montana Bureau of Mines and Geology, 2010, Groundwater Assessment Program Fact Sheet, 4 p. (accessed March 8, 2012, at *http://www.mbmg.mtech.edu/pdf/ground-WaterAssessmentReport-dec2010.pdf*).   R

Nimick, D.A., Brooks, Tom, Dodge, K.A., and Tuck, L.K., 1993, Hydrology and water chemistry of shallow aquifers along the upper Clark Fork, western Montana: U.S. Geological Survey Water-Resources Investigations Report 93-4052, 63 p. (Available at *http://pubs.er.usgs.gov/publication/wri934052*.)   C,L,Q,S

Noble, R.A., Bergantino, R.N., Patton, T.W., Sholes, B.C., Daniel, F., and Scofield, J., 1982, Occurrence and characteristics of ground water in Montana: Montana Bureau of Mines and Geology Open-File Report 99, 214 p., 48 sheet(s).

Patton, T.W., 2006, Water levels and climate, drought monitoring report: Montana Bureau of Mines and Geology, 21 p. (accessed March 8, 2012, at *http://mbmggwic.mtech.edu/sqlserver/v11/reports/pdf/drought2006july.pdf*).   L,R

Patton, T.W., and McKenna, D.P., compilers, 1996, Generalized map showing the distribution of aquifers and water wells in the upper Clark Fork River basin: Montana Bureau of Mines and Geology Ground-Water Open-File Report 1, 1 sheet(s), 1:250,000 (accessed March 8, 2012, at *http://mbmggwic.mtech.edu/gwcpmaps/gwof01untiled.pdf*).   G,R

Patton, T.W., Smith, L.N., and LaFave, J.I., 2003, Ground-water resources of the Flathead Lake area: Flathead, Lake, Sanders, and Missoula Counties, Montana: Montana Bureau of Mines and Geology Information Pamphlet No. 4, 4 p. (Available at *http://www.mbmg.mtech.edu/pdf/IP_4.pdf*.) G,R

Parrett, Charles, and Johnson, D.R., 1990, Montana water supply and use, *in* Carr, J.F, Chase, E.R., Paulson, R.W., and Moody, D.W., compilers, National water summary 1987—Hydrologic events and water supply and use: U.S. Geological Survey Water-Supply Paper 2350, p. 337-344. (Available at*http://pubs.er.usgs.gov/publication/wsp2350*.) R,U

Reed, T.E., and McMurtrey, R.G., 1970, Water levels and artesian pressures in observation wells in Montana, 1966-69: Montana Bureau of Mines and Geology Bulletin 76, 36 p. L

Slagle, S.E., 1992, Irrigation-canal leakage in the Flathead Indian Reservation, northwestern Montana: U.S. Geological Survey Water-Resources Investigations Report 92-4066, 77 p. (Available at *http://pubs.er.usgs.gov/publication/wri924066*.) D,G,H,K,L

Slagle, S.E., 1988, Geohydrology of the Flathead Indian Reservation, northwestern Montana: U.S. Geological Survey Water-Resources Investigations Report 88-4142, 119 p. (Available at *http://pubs.er.usgs.gov/publication/wri884142*.) C,D,G,H, K,L,Q

Smith, L.N., 2006, Hydrologic framework of the Lolo-Bitterroot Area ground-water characterization study (open-file version): Montana Bureau of Mines and Geology Ground-Water Assessment Atlas 4B-02, 1 sheet(s), 1:250,000 (accessed March 8, 2012, at *http://mbmggwic.mtech.edu/gwcpmaps/gwaa04map02untiled.pdf*). D,G

Smith, L.N., 2006, Thickness of quaternary unconsolidated deposits in the Lolo-Bitterroot area, Mineral, Missoula, and Ravalli Counties, Montana (open-file version): Montana Bureau of Mines and Geology Ground-Water Assessment Atlas 4B-03, 1 sheet(s), 1:125,000 (accessed March 8, 2012, at *http://mbmggwic.mtech.edu/gwcpmaps/gwaa04map03untiled.pdf*). G

Smith, L.N., 2006, Altitude of the bedrock surface, Mineral and Missoula Counties, Montana (open-file version): Montana Bureau of Mines and Geology Ground-Water Assessment Atlas 4B-04, 1 sheet(s), 1:150,000 (accessed March 8, 2012, at *http://mbmggwic.mtech.edu/gwcpmaps/gwaa04map04untiled.pdf*). G

Smith, L.N., 2006, Altitude of the bedrock surface in the Bitterroot Valley: Missoula and Ravalli Counties, Montana (open-file version): Montana Bureau of Mines and Geology Ground-Water Assessment Atlas 4B-05, 1 sheet(s), 1:125,000 (accessed March 8, 2012, at *http://mbmggwic.mtech.edu/gwcpmaps/gwaa04map05untiled.pdf*). G

Smith, L.N., 2006, Patterns of water-level fluctuations, Lolo-Bitterroot area, Mineral, Missoula, and Ravalli Counties, Montana (open-file version): Montana Bureau of Mines and Geology Ground-Water Assessment Atlas 4B-10, 1 sheet(s), 1:350,000 (accessed March 8, 2012, at *http://mbmggwic.mtech.edu/gwcpmaps/gwaa04map10untiled.pdf*). L

Smith, L.N., LaFave, J.I., Carstarphen, C.A., Mason, D.J., and Richter, M.G., 2000, Ground-water resources of the Flathead Lake Area: Flathead, Lake, and parts of Missoula and Sanders Counties. Part B- Maps (open-file versions): Montana Bureau of Mines and Geology Ground-Water Assessment Atlas 2B, 11 sheet(s). C,D,G,L

Uthman, W., Waren, K., and Corbett, M., 2000, A reconnaissance ground water investigation in the upper Flathead River valley area: Montana Bureau of Mines and Geology Open-File Report 414, 151 p. (accessed March 8, 2012, at *http://www.mbmg.mtech.edu/pdf-open-files/MBMG414-upperflathead.pdf*).   C,D,L,Q

Waren, K.B., and Patton, T.W., 2007, Ground-water resource development in the Flathead Lake ground-water characterization area, Flathead, Lake, Missoula, and Sanders Counties, Montana: Montana Bureau of Mines and Geology Ground-Water Open-File Report 19, 2 sheet(s). (accessed March 8, 2012, at *http://mbmggwic.mtech.edu/gwcpmaps/gwof19_1untiled.pdf* and *http://mbmggwic.mtech.edu/gwcpmaps/gwof19_2untiled.pdf*).   G,L,R,U

Waren, K.B., and Patton, T.W., 2007, Ground-water resource development in the Lolo-Bitterroot ground-water characterization area, Mineral, Missoula, and Ravalli Counties, Montana: Montana Bureau of Mines and Geology Ground-Water Open-File Report 20, 2 sheet(s). (accessed March 8, 2012, at *http://mbmggwic.mtech.edu/gwcpmaps/gwof20_1untiled.pdf* and *http://mbmggwic.mtech.edu/gwcpmaps/gwof20_2untiled.pdf*).   G,L,R,U

Wilke, K.R., 1979, Selected well inventory and chemical analyses of groundwater, parts of Missoula and Powell Counties, Montana: U.S. Geological Survey Open-File Report 79-1491, 4 p. (Available at *http://pubs.er.usgs.gov/publication/ofr791491*.)   C,L

Wilke, K.R., 1976, Groundwater levels and chemical quality of groundwater in Lincoln, Montana: U.S. Geological Survey Open-File Report 76-333, 4 sheets. (Available at *http://pubs.er.usgs.gov/publication/ofr76333*.)   C,L,R

Washington

Citation	Information codes
Ader, M.J., 1996, Hydrogeology of the Green Bluff plateau, Spokane County, Washington: Washington Department of Ecology Open-File Technical Report 96-3, 1 v.	D,G,H,L,S
Anderson, H.W., Jr., 1968, Ground-water resources of Island County, Washington: Washington State Department of Water Resources, Water-Supply Bulletin No. 25, Part II, p. 35-317 (accessed March 8, 2012, at *http://www.ecy.wa.gov/programs/eap/wsb/wsb_All.html#p25*).	C,D,H,L,U
Anderson, Randall, 1986, Hydrogeologic study of the Deer Park, Washington aquifer system: Eastern Washington University, Cheney, M.S. thesis, 80 p., 7 pls.	G,H,K,Q
Artim, E.R., 1975, Ground water in the Methow Valley, Mazama to Winthrop: Washington Division of Geology and Earth Resources Open-File Report 75-1, 9 p., 4 pls. (accessed March 8, 2012, at *http://www.dnr.wa.gov/publications/ger_ofr75-1_groundwater_methow_valley_pt1.pdf* and *http://www.dnr.wa.gov/publications/ger_ofr75-1_groundwater_methow_valley_pt2.pdf*).	D,G,L

Bauer, H.H., and Mastin, M.C., 1997, Recharge from precipitation in three small glacial - till - mantled catchments in the Puget Sound lowland, Washington: U.S. Geological Survey Water-Resources Investigations Report 96-4219, 119 p. (Available at *http://pubs.er.usgs.gov/publication/wri964219*.)   B,C,D,G, H,L,M

Bidlake, W.R., and Payne, K.L., 2001, Estimating recharge to groundwater from precipitation at Naval Submarine Base Bangor and vicinity, Kitsap County, Washington: U.S. Geological Survey Water-Resources Investigations Report 01-4110, 33 p. (Available at *http://pubs.er.usgs.gov/publication/wri014110*.)   B

Boese, R.M., 1996, Aquifer delineation and baseline groundwater quality investigation of a portion of north Spokane County, Washington: Cheney, Eastern Washington University, M.S. thesis, 224 p.   C,D,G,H, K,L,Q,S

Boleneus, D.E., and Derkey, R.E., 1996, Geohydrology of Peone Prairie, Spokane County, Washington: Washington Geology, v. 24, no. 1, p. 30-39 (accessed March 8, 2012, at *http://www.dnr.wa.gov/Publications/ger_washington_geology_1996_v24_no1.pdf*).   C,D,G,L

Bolke, E.L., and Vaccaro, J.J., 1979, Selected hydrologic data for Spokane Valley, Spokane, Washington, 1977-78: U.S. Geological Survey Open-File Report 79-333, 98 p., 1 pl. (Available at *http://pubs.er.usgs.gov/publication/ofr79333*.)   C,D,L

Brown and Caldwell, 1985, Clover/Chambers Creek geohydrologic study: Seattle, Washington, Brown and Caldwell, Final report: Tacoma-Pierce County Health Department, 1 v.   B,C,D,G, H,L,K,Q,U

Byers, H.G., 1902, The water resources of Washington: Potable and mineral water: Washington Geological Survey Annual Report for 1901, v. 1, part v., 11 p. (accessed March 8, 2012, at *http://www.dnr.wa.gov/publications/ger_ar1901_v1_pt5.pdf*).   C,G,H,Q

Carey, B.M., 2003, Groundwater/surface water interactions in the Upper Sammamish River: A preliminary analysis: Washington Department of Ecology Publication No. 03-03-015, 25 p. (accessed March 8, 2012, at *http://www.ecy.wa.gov/pubs/0303015.pdf*).   D,H,L

Cline, D.R., 1974, A ground-water investigation of the Lummi Indian Reservation area, Washington: U.S. Geological Survey Open-File Report 74-1016, 66 p. (Available at *http://pubs.er.usgs.gov/publication/ofr741016*.)   C,D,G,H, K,L,Q

Cline, D.R., 1969, Ground-water resources and related geology, north central Spokane and southeastern Stevens Counties, Washington: Washington Department of Water Resources Water Supply Bulletin 27, 195 p., 2 pls. (accessed March 8, 2012, at *http://www.ecy.wa.gov/programs/eap/wsb/wsb_All.html#p27*) .   C,D,G,H, L,Q,U

Cline, D.R., 1969, Availability of ground water in the Federal Way area, King County, Washington: U.S. Geological Survey Open-File Report 69-44, 60 p. (Available at *http://pubs.er.usgs.gov/publication/ofr6944*.)   B,D,G,H,L

Cline, D.R., Jones, M.A., Dion, N.P., Whiteman, K.J., and Sapik, D.B., 1982, Preliminary survey of ground-water resources for Island County, Washington: U.S. Geological Survey Open-File Report 82-561, 46 p. (Available at *http://pubs.er.usgs.gov/publication/ofr82561*.)   D,G,H,Q

Cox, S.E., 2003, Estimates of residence time and related variations in quality of ground water beneath Submarine Base Bangor and vicinity, Kitsap County, Washington: U.S. Geological Survey Water-Resources Investigations Report 03-4058, 53 p. (Available at *http://pubs.er.usgs.gov/publication/wri034058.*) — C,D,G, H,L,Q

Cox, S.E., Simonds, F.W., Huffman, R.L., Doremus, Llyn, and Defawe, R.M., 2005, Ground water/surface water interactions and quality of discharging ground-water in streams of the Lower Nooksack River Basin, Whatcom County, Washington: U.S. Geological Survey Scientific Investigations Report 2005-5255, 46 p. (Available at *http://pubs.er.usgs.gov/publication/sir20055255.*) — C,D,H,Q

Culhane, Tom, Kelly, Alice, and Liszak, J.L., 1995, Initial watershed assessment, Water Resources Inventory Area 9, Green-Duwamish watershed; Draft: Washington Department of Ecology Open-File Report 95-01, 52 p. (accessed March 8, 2012, at *http://www.ecy.wa.gov/pubs/95001.pdf*). — G,H,U,Q

Dames and Moore, Inc., and Cosmopolitan Engineering Group, 1995, Draft initial watershed assessment Water Resources Inventory Area 55, Little Spokane River watershed: Dames and Moore, Inc., and Cosmopolitan Engineering Group Open-File Technical Report 95-15, 33 p. — R

Dames and Moore, Inc., and Cosmopolitan Engineering Group, 1995, Initial watershed assessment, Water Resources Inventory Area 60, Kettle River watershed—Draft: Washington State Department of Ecology Open-File Report 95-16, 1 v. — R

Dames and Moore, Inc., and Cosmopolitan Engineering Group, 1995, Initial watershed assessment, Water Resources Inventory Area 62, Pend Oreille River watershed—Draft: Washington State Department of Ecology Open-File Report 95-17, 1 v. — R

Didricksen, Kayti, 2001, Hydrogeologic assessment of the Swinomish Indian Reservation, Skagit County, Washington: Eastern Washington University, M.S. thesis, 109 p. (Abstract accessed March 8, 2012, at *http://www.geology.ewu.edu/dept/kdidrick.html.*) — C,D,G, H,L,Q

Dinicola, R.S., 2005, Hydrogeology and trichloroethene contamination in the sea-level aquifer beneath the Logistics Center, Fort Lewis, Washington: U.S. Geological Survey Scientific Investigations Report 2005-5035, 50 p. (Available at *http://pubs.er.usgs.gov/publication/sir20055035.*) — C,D,G, H,L,Q

Dion, N.P., and Lum, W.E., II, 1977, Municipal, industrial, and irrigation water use in Washington, 1975: U.S. Geological Survey Open-File Report 77-308, 34 p. (Available at *http://pubs.er.usgs.gov/publication/ofr77308.*) — U

Dion, N.P., Olsen, T.D., and Payne, K.L., 1988, Preliminary evaluation of the ground-water resources of Bainbridge Island, Kitsap County, Washington: U.S. Geological Survey Water-Resources Investigations Report 87-4237, 82 p. (Available at *http://pubs.er.usgs.gov/publication/wri874237.*) — C,D,G,H, K,L,Q,U

Dion, N.P., and Sumioka, S.S., 1984, Seawater intrusion into Coastal Aquifers: Washington State Department of Ecology Water-Supply Bulletin No. 56, 24 p. (accessed March 8, 2012, at *http://www.ecy.wa.gov/programs/eap/wsb/pdfs/WSB_56_Book.pdf*). — C,D,H,Q

Dion, N.P., Walters, K.L., and Nelson, L.M., 1980, Water resources of the Makah Indian Reservation, Washington: U.S. Geological Survey Water-Resources Investigations Report 80-15, 54 p. (Available at *http://pubs.er.usgs.gov/publication/wri8015.*) — C,D,G,L, Q,S

Dragovich, J.D., Grisamer, C.L., 1998, Quaternary stratigraphy, cross sections, and general geohydrologic potential of the Bow and Alger 7.5-minute quadrangles, western Skagit County, Washington: Washington Division of Geology and Earth Resources Open-File Report 98-8, 29 p., 6 pls. (accessed March 8, 2012, at *http://www.dnr.wa.gov/Publications/ger_ofr98-8_quat_strat_bow_alger.zip*). — D,G,H

Drost, B.W., 1996, Selected ground-water data for the Lummi Indian Reservation, Whatcom County, Washington, 1995: U.S. Geological Survey Open-File Report 96-166, 21 p. (Available at *http://pubs.er.usgs.gov/publication/ofr96166.*) — C,D,L

Drost, B.W., 1986, Water resources of Clallam County, Washington: Phase 1 report: U.S. Geological Survey Water-Resources Investigations Report 83-4227, 263 p. (Available at *http://pubs.er.usgs.gov/publication/wri834227.*) — C,D,H,L, Q,U

Drost, B.W., 1985, Appraisal of ground-water conditions and potential for seawater intrusion at Taholah, Quinault Indian Reservation, Washington: U.S. Geological Survey Water-Resources Investigations Report 84-4361, 26 p. (Available at *http://pubs.er.usgs.gov/publication/wri844361.*) — C,D,H, L,Q

Drost, B.W., 1983, Impact of changes in land use on the ground-water system in the Sequim-Dungeness Peninsula, Clallam County, Washington: U.S. Geological Survey Water-Resources Investigations Report 83-4094, 61 p. (Available at *http://pubs.er.usgs.gov/publication/wri834094.*) — B,C,D,G, H,K,L,M, Q,U

Drost, B.W., 1983, Water resources of the Tulalip Indian Reservation, Washington: U.S. Geological Survey Open-File Report 82-648, 153 p. (Available at *http://pubs.er.usgs.gov/publication/ofr82648.*) — B,C,D,G, H,L,Q,S,U

Drost, B.W., 1982, Water resources of the Gig Harbor Peninsula and adjacent areas, Washington: U.S. Geological Survey Open-File Report 81-1021, 148 p. (Available at *http://pubs.er.usgs.gov/publication/ofr811021.*) — B,C,D,G, H,L,Q,S,U

Drost, B.W., 1979, Progress report on water resources of the Tulalip Indian Reservation, Washington: U.S. Geological Survey Water-Resources Investigations Report 78-31, 39 p. (Available at *http://pubs.er.usgs.gov/publication/wri7831.*) — C,D,G,L, Q,S

Drost, B.W., 1979, Water resources of the Swinomish Indian Reservation, Washington: U.S. Geological Survey Water-Resources Investigations Report 79-12, 83 p. (Available at *http://pubs.er.usgs.gov/publication/wri7912.*) — D

Drost, B.W., 1977, Preliminary assessment of the water resources of the Tulalip Indian Reservation, Washington: U.S. Geological Survey Open-File Report 76-493, 89 p. (Available at *http://pubs.er.usgs.gov/publication/ofr76493.*) — C,D,L,Q

Drost, B.W., Ely, D.M., and Lum, W.E. II, 1999, Conceptual model and numerical simulation of the ground-water-flow system in the unconsolidated sediments of Thurston County, Washington: U.S. Geological Survey Water-Resources Investigations Report 99-4165, 254 p. (Available at *http://pubs.er.usgs.gov/publication/wri994165.*) — B,D,G,H, K,L,M,U

Drost, B.W., and Lombard, R.E., 1978, Water in the Skagit River basin, Washington: Washington State Department of Ecology Water-Supply Bulletin No. 47, 247 p. (accessed March 8, 2012, at *http://www.ecy.wa.gov/programs/eap/wsb/wsb_All.html#p47*). · B,C,D,G, H,L,Q,S,U

Drost, B.W., Turney, G.L., Dion, N.P., and Jones, M.A., 1998, Hydrology and quality of ground water in northern Thurston County: U.S. Geological Survey Water-Resources Investigations Report 92-4109 [revised], 230 p. (Available at *http://pubs.er.usgs.gov/publication/wri924109.*) · B,C,D,G, H,K,L,Q,U

Ebbert, J.C., 1984, The quality of ground water in the principal aquifers of northeastern-north central Washington: U.S. Geological Survey Water-Resources Investigations Report 83-4102, 112 p. (Available at *http://pubs.er.usgs.gov/publication/wri834102.*) · C,D,Q

Ebbert, J.C., Bortleson, G.C., Fuste, L.A., and Prych, E.A., 1987, Water quality in the lower Puyallup River valley and adjacent uplands, Pierce County, Washington: U.S. Geological Survey Water-Resources Investigations Report 86-4154, 199 p. (Available at *http://pubs.er.usgs.gov/publication/wri864154.*) · C,D,G,H, Q,S,U

Ebbert, J.C., Embrey, S.S., Black, R.W., Tesoriero, A.J., and Haggland, A.L., 2000, Water quality in the Puget Sound Basin, Washington and British Columbia, 1996–98: U.S. Geological Survey Circular 1216, 31 p. (Available at *http://pubs.er.usgs.gov/publication/cir1216.*) · C,D,Q,S,U

Economic and Engineering Services, Inc., 1989, Island County ground water management plan; Part A, Technical memorandum—Hydrogeologic characterization and background data collection relating to groundwater protection and management: Economic and Engineering Services, Inc., 1 v. · B,C,D,G, H,K,L,Q,U

Eddy, P.A., 1971, Geology and ground water resources in vicinity of Silverdale, Kitsap County, Washington: Washington State Department of Ecology, Office of Technical Services, 11 p. (accessed March 8, 2012, at *http://www.ecy.wa.gov/pubs/7111006.pdf*). · D,L

Ely, D.M., 2006, Analysis of the sensitivity of simulated recharge to selected parameters for seven watersheds modeled using the precipitation-runoff modeling system: U.S. Geological Survey Scientific Investigations Report 2006-5041, 21 p. (Available at *http://pubs.er.usgs.gov/publication/sir20065041.*) · M

Ely, D.M., 2003, Precipitation-runoff simulations of current and natural streamflow conditions in the Methow River watershed, Washington: U.S. Geological Survey Water-Resources Investigations Report 03-4246, 35 p. (Available at *http://pubs.er.usgs.gov/publication/wri034246.*) · B,M,S

Ely, D.M., and Kahle, S.C., 2004, Conceptual model and numerical simulation of the groundwater-flow system in the unconsolidated deposits of the Colville River watershed, Stevens County, Washington: U.S. Geological Survey Scientific Investigations Report 2004-5237, 73 p. (Available at *http://pubs.er.usgs.gov/publication/sir20045237.*) · B,D,G,H, K,M

Embrey, S.S., Hansen, A.J., and Cline, D.R., 1997, Ground-water resources of three areas on the Spokane and Kalispel Indian Reservations, northeastern Washington: U.S. Geological Survey Water-Resources Investigations Report 94-4235, 67 p., 1 pl. (Available at *http://pubs.er.usgs.gov/publication/wri944235.*) · C,D,G,H, K,L,Q

Embrey, S.S., and Jones, J.L., 1998, Reconnaissance hydrogeology and water quality of the Swinomish Indian Reservation, Skagit County, Washington: U.S. Geological Survey Water-Resources Investigations Report 96-4031, 28 p. (Available at *http://pubs.er.usgs.gov/publication/wri964031.*)   C,D,G,H, K,L,Q,R,U

EMCON, 1992, Deer Park ground water characterization study, hydrogeologic summary report, v. 1: Bothell, Washington, EMCON Northwest, Inc., project 0622-001.02, 83 p.   B,C,D,G, H,L

Evans, S.H., and Jensen, R.E., 1996, Geohydrologic review of the Cedar River ground-water basin: Washington Geology, v. 24, no. 4, p. 3-13. (accessed March 8, 2012, at *http://www.dnr.wa.gov/Publications/ger_washington_geology_1996_v24_no4.pdf*).   D,G,R

Fabritz, Jason, Massmann, Joel, and Booth, D.B., 1998, Duwamish basin groundwater pathways—Development of a three-dimensional, numerical groundwater flow model for the Duwamish River basin: University of Washington Department of Civil and Environmental Engineering, 59 p.   B,D,G,H, K,M

Fasser, E.T., and Julich, R.J., 2010, Groundwater Levels for Selected Wells in the Chehalis River Basin, Washington: U.S. Geological Survey Data Series 512. (Available at *http://pubs.er.usgs.gov/publication/ds512.*)   D,L

Fasser, E.T., and Julich, R.J., 2009, Hydrographs showing ground-water level changes for selected wells in the Lower Skagit River Basin, Washington: U.S. Geological Survey Data Series 441. (Available at *http://pubs.er.usgs.gov/publication/ds441.*)   D,L

Frank, D.G., 1980, Availability, distribution, and uses of data from wells, springs, and test holes in the Port Townsend quadrangle, Puget Sound region, Washington: U.S. Geological Survey Open-File Report 80-430, 1 pl., scale 1:100,000 (Available at *http://pubs.er.usgs.gov/publication/ofr80430.*)   D

Frans, L.M., Bachmann, M.P., Sumioka, S.S., and Olsen, T.D., 2011, Conceptual model and numerical simulation of the groundwater-flow system of Bainbridge Island, Washington: U.S. Geological Survey Scientific Investigations Report 2011–5021, 96 p. (Available at *http://pubs.er.usgs.gov/publication/sir20115021.*)   B,D,G, H,K,M

Frans, L.M., and Kresch, D.L., 2004, Water resources of the Tulalip Indian Reservation and adjacent area, Snohomish County, Washington, 2001-03: U.S. Geological Survey Scientific Investigations Report 2004-5166, 86 p. (Available at *http://pubs.er.usgs.gov/publication/sir20045166.*)   B,D,G,H, K,L,U

Foxworthy, B.L., 1979, Summary appraisals of the nation's ground - water resources - Pacific Northwest region: U.S. Geological Survey Professional Paper 813-S, 39 p. (Available at *http://pubs.er.usgs.gov/publication/pp813S.*)   B,D,H, L,Q

Garling, M.E., Molenaar, Dee, and others, 1965, Water resources and geology of the Kitsap Peninsula and certain adjacent Islands: Washington State Department of Conservation, Division of Water Resources, Water-Supply Bulletin No. 18, 309 p. (accessed March 8, 2012, at *http://www.ecy.wa.gov/programs/eap/wsb/wsb_All.html#p18*).   C,D,G,H, L,Q,S,U

Garrigues, R.S., and Carey, B.M., 1999, Groundwater data compilation for the Okanogan Watershed: Washington State Department of Ecology Publication No. 99-342, 114 p. (accessed March 8, 2012, at *http://www.ecy.wa.gov/pubs/99342.pdf*).   C,H,Q

Garrigues, R.S., and Litman, T., 1990, Lopez Island test/observation well completion report: Washington State Department of Ecology Publication No. OFTR 90-03, 18 p. (accessed March 8, 2012, at *http://www.ecy.wa.gov/pubs/oftr9003.pdf*). — C,D,G, H,Q

Garrigues, R.S., Sinclair, K., and Tooley, J., 1998, Chehalis River watershed surficial aquifer characterization: Washington State Department of Ecology Publication No. 98-335, 33 p. (accessed March 8, 2012, at *http://www.ecy.wa.gov/pubs/98335.pdf*). — G,H,Q

Gelinas, Sharon, 2000, An exploratory statistical analysis of the ground water in the Abbotsford-Sumas aquifer: Bellingham, Western Washington University, M.S. thesis, 184 p. — C,Q

Golder Associates, Inc., 2004, Final report to the Little and Middle Spokane watershed WRIA 55 and 57 planning unit, level 2 technical assessment—Watershed simulation model: Seattle, Golder Associates, Inc., prepared under grant no. 9800300, from the Washington State Department of Ecology, February 14, 2004, 51 p., 4 appendixes. — B,G,H,K, L,M

Golder Associates, Inc., 2003, Little Spokane (WRIA 55) and Middle Spokane (WRIA 57) watershed planning phase II–Level 1 assessment, data compilation and analysis: Seattle, Golder Associates, Inc., prepared under grant no. 9800300 from the Washington State Department of Ecology, variously paginated. — B,C,D,G, H,L,Q,U

Greene, K.E., 1997, Ambient quality of ground water in the vicinity of naval submarine base Bangor, Kitsap County, Washington: U.S. Geological Survey Water-Resources Investigations Report 96-4309, 46 p. (Available at *http://pubs.er.usgs.gov/publication/wri964309.*) — C,D,G,H,Q

Griffin, W.C., Sceva, J.E., Swenson, H.A., and Mundorff, M.J., 1962, Water resources of the Tacoma area, Washington: U.S. Geological Survey Water-Supply Paper 1499-B. [Also published as State of Washington, Department of Conservation, Division of Water Resources, Water-Supply Bulletin No. 19], p. B1-B101. (Available at *http://pubs.er.usgs.gov/publication/wsp1499B* and accessed March 8, 2012, at *http://www.ecy.wa.gov/programs/eap/wsb/wsb_All.html#p19*). — C,D,K,L,Q

Grimstad, P., 1975, A geohydrologic reconnaissance of Point Roberts Area, Whatcom County, Washington: Washington State Department of Ecology Publication No. OFTR 75-02, 16 p. (accessed March 8, 2012, at *http://www.ecy.wa.gov/pubs/oftr7502.pdf*). — G,H

Grimstad, Peder, 1971, Geology and ground water resources, Lake McMurray area, Snohomish and Skagit Counties, Washington: Washington State Department of Ecology Technical Report 71-19, 30 p. — G,H,K,L

Grimstad, Peder, and Carson, R.J., 1981, Geology and ground-water resources of eastern Jefferson County, Washington: Washington State Department of Ecology Water-Supply Bulletin no. 54, 125 p., 3 pls. (accessed March 8, 2012, at *http://www.ecy.wa.gov/programs/eap/wsb/pdfs/WSB_54_Book.pdf*; *http://www.ecy.wa.gov/programs/eap/wsb/pdfs/WSB_54_Plates.pdf*). — D,G,H,L

Hansen, A.J., Jr., and Bolke, E.L., 1980, Ground-water availability on the Kitsap Peninsula, Washington: U.S. Geological Survey Open-File Report 80-1186, 65 p. (Available at *http://pubs.er.usgs.gov/publication/ofr801186.*) — G,H,Q

Harkness, R.E., Myers, D.A., and Bortleson, G.C., 1974, Water resources of the Colville Indian Reservation, Washington: U.S. Geological Survey Open-File Report 74-1045, 149 p. (Available at *http://pubs.er.usgs.gov/publication/ofr741045.*) — R,S

Huffman, R.L., 2000, Selected ground-water data for the Logistics Center, Fort Lewis, Washington, 1997–1998: U.S. Geological Survey Open-File Report 00-149, 76 p. (Available at *http://pubs.er.usgs.gov/publication/ofr00149.*)   D,C,L,Q

Johnson, K.H., and Savoca, M.E., 2010, Numerical simulation of the groundwater-flow system in tributary subbasins and vicinity, lower Skagit River basin, Skagit and Snohomish Counties, Washington: U.S. Geological Survey Scientific Investigations Report 2010-5184, 78 p. (Available at *http://pubs.er.usgs.gov/publication/sir20105184.*)   B,D,G,H, K,L,M

Johnson, K.H., Savoca, M.E., and Clothier, Burt, 2011, Numerical simulation of the groundwater-flow system in the Chambers-Clover Creek Watershed and Vicinity, Pierce County, Washington: U.S. Geological Survey Scientific Investigations Report 2011–5086, 108 p. (Available at *http://pubs.er.usgs.gov/publication/sir20115086.*)   B,D,G,H, K,L,M

Johnson, M.S., 1992, Hydrology and hydrogeology of Long Lake, Spokane and Stevens Counties, Washington: Cheney, Eastern Washington University, M.S.thesis, 222 p.   B,D,G,H, L,S

Jones, M.A., 1996, Delineation of hydrogeologic units in the lower Dungeness River basin, Clallam County, Washington: U.S. Geological Survey Water-Resources Investigations Report 95-4008, 11 p. (Available at *http://pubs.er.usgs.gov/publication/wri954008.*)   D,G

Jones, M.A., 1985, Occurrence of ground water and potential for seawater intrusion, Island County, Washington: U.S. Geological Survey Water-Resources Investigations Report 85-4046, 6 sheets. (Available at *http://pubs.er.usgs.gov/publication/wri854046.*)   D,G,H, Q,U

Jones, M.A., Jones, J.L., and Olsen, T.D., 2000, Ground-water flooding in glacial terrain of southern Puget Sound, Washington: U.S. Geological Survey Fact Sheet FS-111-00, 4 p. (Available at *http://pubs.er.usgs.gov/publication/fs11100.*)   G

Jones, M.A., Orr, L.A., Ebbert, J.C., and Sumioka, S.S., 1999, Ground-water hydrology of the Tacoma–Puyallup area, Pierce County, Washington: U.S. Geological Survey Water-Resources Investigations Report 99-4013, 154 p. (Available at *http://pubs.er.usgs.gov/publication/wri994013.*)   B,C,D,G, H,K,L,Q

Justin, G.B., Julich, R.J., and Payne, K.L., 2009, Hydrographs showing groundwater level changes for selected wells in the Chambers-Clover Creek watershed and vicinity, Pierce County, Washington: U.S. Geological Survey Data Series 453 (Available at *http://pubs.er.usgs.gov/publication/ds453.*)   D

Kahle, S.C., 1998, Hydrogeology of Naval Submarine Base Bangor and vicinity, Kitsap County, Washington: U.S. Geological Survey Water-Resources Investigations Report 97-4060, 107 p. (Available at *http://pubs.er.usgs.gov/publication/wri974060.*)   G,H,K,L

Kahle, S.C., 1990, Hydrostratigraphy and groundwater flow in the Sumas area, Whatcom County, Washington: Bellingham, Western Washington University, M.S. thesis, 92 p.   D,G,H,L

Kahle, S.C., Longpre, C.I., Smith, R.R., Sumioka, S.S., Watkins, A.M., and Kresch, D.L., 2003, Water resources in the groundwater system in unconsolidated deposits of the Colville River watershed, Stevens County, Washington: U.S. Geological Survey Water-Resources Investigations Report 03-4128, 76 p. (Available at *http://pubs.er.usgs.gov/publication/wri034128.*)   B,C,D, G,H,K,L, S,U

Kahle, S.C., and Olsen, T.D., 1995, Hydrogeology and quality of ground water on Guemes Island, Skagit County, Washington: U.S. Geological Survey Water-Resources Investigations Report 94-4236, 83 p. (Available at *http://pubs.er.usgs.gov/publication/wri944236*.)   B,C,D,G, H,K,L,Q,U

Kahle, S.C., Taylor, W.A., Lin, Sonja, Sumioka, S.S., and Olsen, T.D., 2010, groundwater and surface-water systems, land use, pumpage, and water budget of the Chamokane Creek basin, Stevens County, Washington: U.S. Geological Survey Scientific Investigations Report 2010-5165, 60 p. (Available at *http://pubs.er.usgs.gov/publication/sir20105165*.)   B,D,G,H, K,L,S,U

Kimmel, G.E., 1963, Contamination of ground water by sea-water intrusion along Puget Sound, Washington–An area having abundant precipitation: U.S. Geological Survey Professional Paper 475-B, p. 182-185. (Available at *http://pubs.er.usgs.gov/publication/pp475B*.)   C,R,Q

Kimmel, R.S., 1982, Groundwater in the Nooksack lowland of western Whatcom County, Washington: Bellingham, Western Washington University, B.S. thesis, 62 p.   G,H,L,R

Konrad, C.P., Drost, B.W., and Wagner, R.J., 2003, Hydrogeology of the unconsolidated sediments, water quality, and ground-water/surface-water exchanges in the Methow River basin Okanogan County, Washington: U.S. Geological Survey Water-Resources Investigations Report 03-4244, 137 p. (Available at *http://pubs.er.usgs.gov/publication/wri034244*.)   B,C,D,G, H,K,L,Q,S

Laird, L.B., and Walters, K.L., 1967, Municipal, industrial, and irrigation water use in Washington, 1965: U.S. Geological Survey Open-File Report 67-142, 13 p. (Available at *http://pubs.er.usgs.gov/publication/ofr67142*.)   U

Landes, Henry, 1905, Preliminary report on the underground waters of Washington: U.S. Geological Survey Water-Supply Paper 111, 85 p. (Available at *http://pubs.er.usgs.gov/publication/wsp111*.)   R

Lane, R.C., 2010, Water use trends in Washington: 1985–2005: U.S. Geological Survey Fact Sheet 2010-3057, 4 p. (Available at *http://pubs.er.usgs.gov/publication/fs20103057*.)   U

Lane, R.C., 2009, Estimated water use in Washington, 2005: U.S. Geological Survey Scientific Investigations Report 2009-5128, 30 p. (Available at *http://pubs.er.usgs.gov/publication/sir20095128*.)   U

Lane, R.C., 2004, Availability of ground-water data for Washington, 2004: U.S. Geological Survey Fact Sheet 2004-3122, 2 p. (Available at *http://pubs.er.usgs.gov/publication/fs20043122*.)   R

Lane, R.C., 2004, Estimated domestic, irrigation, and industrial water use in Washington, 2000: U.S. Geological Survey Scientific Investigations Report 2004-5015, 16 p. (Available at *http://pubs.er.usgs.gov/publication/sir20045015*.)   U

Larson, A.G., and Marti, P.B., 1996, Relationship between ground water and surface water in the Quilceda Creek watershed: Washington State Department of Ecology Publication No. 96-333, 56 p. (accessed March 8, 2012, at *http://www.ecy.wa.gov/pubs/96333.pdf*).   C,G,H,K, L,Q,S

Liesch, B.A., 1955, Records of wells, water levels, and quality of ground water, Sammamish Lake area, King County, Washington: U.S. Geological Survey Open-File Report 55-96, 193 p. (Available at *http://pubs.er.usgs.gov/publication/ofr5596*.)   C,D,L

23

Liesch, B.A., Price, C.E., and Walters, K.L., 1963, Geology and ground-water resources of northwestern King County, Washington: Washington State Department of Conservation, Division of Water Resources, Water-Supply Bulletin No. 20, 241 p. (accessed March 8, 2012, at *http://www.ecy.wa.gov/programs/eap/wsb/wsb_All.html#p20*). — C,D,G, L,Q,U

Lum, W.E., II, 1986, Reconnaissance of the water resources of the Hoh Indian Reservation and the Hoh River basin, Washington: U.S. Geological Survey Water-Resources Investigations Report 85-4018, 56 p. (Available at *http://pubs.er.usgs.gov/publication/wri854018.*) — C,D,L, Q,R,S

Lum, W.E., II, 1984, Availability of ground water from the alluvial aquifer on the Nisqually Indian Reservation, Washington: U.S. Geological Survey Water-Resources Investigations Report 83-4185, 42 p. (Available at *http://pubs.er.usgs.gov/publication/wri834185.*) — C,D,G,H, K,L,M,Q

Lum, W.E., II, 1980, Water resources of the Port Gamble Indian Reservation, Washington: U.S. Geological Survey Water-Resources Investigations Report 79-66, 52 p. (Available at *http://pubs.er.usgs.gov/publication/wri7966.*) — C,D,G,H, L,Q,S,U

Lum, W.E., II, 1979, Water resources of the Port Madison Indian Reservation, Washington: U.S. Geological Survey Water-Resources Investigations 78-112, 73 p. (Available at *http://pubs.er.usgs.gov/publication/wri78112.*) — C,D,G,H, L,Q,S,U

Lum, W.E., II, and Walters, K.L., 1976, Reconnaissance of ground-water resources of the Squaxin Island Indian Reservation, Washington: U.S. Geological Survey Open-File Report 76-382, 49 p. (Available at *http://pubs.er.usgs.gov/publication/ofr76382.*) — B,C,D,G, H,K,L,Q

Luzier, J.E., 1969, Geology and ground-water resources of southwestern King County, Washington: Washington State Department of Water Resources, Water-Supply Bulletin No. 28, 260 p. (accessed March 8, 2012, at *http://www.ecy.wa.gov/programs/eap/wsb/wsb_All.html#p28*). — C,G,H,L, Q,U

Matt, V.J., 1994, Hydrology and hydrogeology of the Spokane Indian Reservation, northeastern Washington State: Cheney, Eastern Washington University, M.S. thesis, 209 p. — D,G,H,K, L,M,S

Milhous, R.T., 1975, A check point report on the Okanogan Basin investigation: Washington State Department of Ecology Publication No. 75-11-008, 21 p. (accessed March 8, 2012, at *http://www.ecy.wa.gov/pubs/7511008.pdf*). — S,U

Molenaar, Dee, 1988, The Spokane aquifer, Washington—Its geologic origin and water-bearing and water-quality characteristics: U.S. Geological Survey Water-Supply Paper 2265, 74 p. (Available at http://pubs.er.usgs.gov/publication/wsp2265.) — G,H,Q,S

Molenaar, Dee, 1961, Flowing artesian wells in Washington State: Washington State Department of Conservation, Division of Water Resources, Water-Supply Bulletin No. 16, 115 p. (Available at *http://www.ecy.wa.gov/programs/eap/wsb/wsb_All.html#p16*). — G,L

Molenaar, Dee, and Cummans, J.E., 1973, Water resources of the Skokomish Indian Reservation, Washington: U.S. Geological Survey Open-File Report 73-192, 58 p. (Available at *http://pubs.er.usgs.gov/publication/ofr73192.*) — C,D,G,L, Q,S

Molenaar, Dee, and Noble, J.B., 1970, Geology and related ground-water occurrence, southeastern Mason County, Washington: Washington State Department of Water Resources, Water-Supply Bulletin No. 29, 145 p. (accessed March 8, 2012, at *http://www.ecy.wa.gov/programs/eap/wsb/wsb_All.html#p29*). — C,D,G,H, L,Q,U

Morgan, D.S., and Jones, J.J., 1999, Numerical model analysis of the effects of ground-water withdrawals on discharge to streams and springs in small basins typical of the Puget Sound Lowland, Washington: U.S. Geological Survey Water-Supply Paper 2492, 73 p. (Available at *http://pubs.er.usgs.gov/publication/wsp2492*.)
    M

Mundorff, M.J., Weigle, J.M., and Holmberg, G.D., 1955, Ground water in the Yelm area, Thurston and Pierce Counties, Washington: U.S. Geological Survey Circular 356, 58 p. (Available at *http://pubs.er.usgs.gov/publication/cir356*; hard copy available at U.S. Geological Survey Menlo Park Library.)
    C,D,G,H, L,Q

Myers, D.A., 1970, Availability of ground water in western Cowlitz County, Washington: State of Washington, Department of Ecology Water-Supply Bulletin No. 35, 63 p. (accessed March 8, 2012, at *http://www.ecy.wa.gov/programs/eap/wsb/wsb_All.html#p35*).
    C,D,G,H, L,Q,S

Myers, D.A., and Cummans, J.E., 1973, Water resources of the Nisqually Indian Reservation, Washington: U.S. Geological Survey Open-File Report 73-201, 30 p. (Available at *http://pubs.er.usgs.gov/publication/ofr73201*.)
    C,D,H, R,S

Newcomb, R.C., 1952, Ground-water resources of Snohomish County, Washington: U.S. Geological Survey Water-Supply Paper 1135, 133 p. (Available at *http://pubs.er.usgs.gov/publication/wsp1135*.)
    C,D,G,H, L,Q,S,U

Newcomb, Reuben, 1933, Underground water of the upper Spokane Valley [student's prize essay]: Pullman, Washington State College [now Washington State University], 16 p., 3 pls. (Original copy available at Washington State University Special Collections Library.)
    D,G,L,R

Newcomb, R.C., Sceva, J.E., and Stromme, Olaf, 1949, Ground-water resources of western Whatcom County, Washington: U.S. Geological Survey Open-File Report 50-7, 134 p. (Available at *http://pubs.er.usgs.gov/publication/ofr407*.)
    C,D,G,H, L,Q

Noble, J.B., 1960, A preliminary report on geology and ground - water resources of the Sequim-Dungeness area, Clallam County, Washington: Washington State Department of Conservation, Division of Water Resources, Water-Supply Bulletin No. 11, 43 p. (accessed March 8, 2012, at *http://www.ecy.wa.gov/programs/eap/wsb/wsb_All.html#p11*).
    C,D,G,H, L,Q

Noble, J.B., and Wallace, E.F., 1966, Geology and ground-water resources of Thurston County, Washington: Washington State Department of Conservation, Division of Water Resources, Water-Supply Bulletin No. 10, v. 2, 141 p. (Available at *http://www.ecy.wa.gov/programs/eap/wsb/wsb_All.html#p10b*).
    C,D,G,H, L,Q,U

Orr, L.A., 2000, Is seawater intrusion affecting ground water on Lopez Island, Washington?: U.S. Geological Survey Fact Sheet FS-057-00, 8 p. (Available at *http://pubs.er.usgs.gov/publication/fs05700*.)
    C,L,Q,R

Orr, L.A., Bauer, H.H, and Wayenberg, J.A., 2002, Estimates of ground - water recharge from precipitation to glacial-deposit and bedrock aquifers on Lopez, San Juan, Orcas, and Shaw Islands, San Juan County, Washington: U.S. Geological Survey Water-Resources Investigations Report 02-4114, 122 p. (Available at *http://pubs.er.usgs.gov/publication/wri024114*.)
    B

Packard, F.A., Sumioka, S.S., and Whiteman, K.J., 1983, Ground water-surface water relationships in the Bonaparte Creek basin, Okanogan County, Washington, 1979-80: U.S. Geological Survey Open-File Report 82-172, 46 p. (Available at *http://pubs.er.usgs.gov/publication/ofr82172.*) — D,G,H, L,S

Parker, G.G., Jr., 1971, Municipal, industrial, and irrigation water use in Washington, 1970: U.S. Geological Survey Open-File Report, 21 p. — U

Pearson, H.E., and Higgins, G.T., 1977, Water resources of the Chehalis Indian Reservation, Washington: U.S. Geological Survey Open-File Report 77-704, 101 p., 4 pls. (Available at *http://pubs.er.usgs.gov/publication/ofr77704.*) — C,D,G, L,S

Perkins, S., 1986, Aquifer characteristics and seawater intrusion of Machaye Harbor Area and Northern Lopez Island, San Juan County, Washington: Washington State Department of Ecology Publication No. OFTR 86-03, 19 p. (accessed March 8, 2012, at *http://www.ecy.wa.gov/pubs/oftr8603.pdf*). — C,D,G, L,Q

Pitz, C.F., and Sinclair, K.A., 1999, Estimated baseflow characteristics of selected Washington rivers and streams: Water Supply Bulletin No. 60: Washington State Department of Ecology Publication No. 99-327, 221 p. (accessed March 8, 2012, at *http://www.ecy.wa.gov/pubs/99327.pdf*). — B

Pitz, C.F., Sinclair, K.A., and Oestreich, A.J., 2005, Washington State Groundwater Assessment Program: Hydrology and quality of groundwater in the Centralia-Chehalis area surficial aquifer: Washington State Department of Ecology Publication No. 05-03-040, 103 p. (accessed March 8, 2012, at *http://www.ecy.wa.gov/biblio/0503040.html*). — C,D,G,H, K,L,Q,S

Pluhowski, E.J., and Thomas, C.A., 1968, A water-balance equation for the Rathdrum Prairie ground-water reservoir, near Spokane, Washington: U.S. Geological Survey Professional Paper 600-D, p. D75 - D78. (Available at *http://pubs.er.usgs.gov/publication/pp600D.*) — B,H

Prych, E.A., 1999, A tracer test to estimate hydraulic conductivities and dispersivities of sediments in the shallow aquifer at the East Gate Disposal Yard, Fort Lewis, Washington: U.S. Geological Survey Water-Resources Investigations Report 99-4244, 48 p. (Available at *http://pubs.er.usgs.gov/publication/wri994244.*) — C,D,G, K,L

Prych, E.A., 1997, Numerical simulation of ground-water flow paths and discharge locations at Puget Sound Naval Shipyard, Bremerton, Washington: U.S. Geological Survey Water-Resources Investigations Report 96-4147, 43 p. (Available at *http://pubs.er.usgs.gov/publication/wri964147.*) — B,D,G, L,M

Richardson, Donald, Bingham, J.W., Madison, R.J., 1968, Water resources of King County, Washington *with a section on* Sediment in streams by R.C. Williams: U.S. Geological Survey Water-Supply Paper 1852, 74 p. (Available at *http://pubs.er.usgs.gov/publication/wsp1852.*) — B,C,D,G, H,L,Q, S,U

Ritzi, R.W., Jr., 1983, The hydrogeologic setting and water resources of Vashon and Maury Islands, King County, Washington: Dayton, Ohio, Wright State University, M.S. thesis, 115 p. — B,C,D,G, H,L,Q,S

Robinson and Noble, Inc., 1987, Description of the aquifer systems in the Federal Way area: Robinson and Noble, Inc., 1 v., 8 pls. — D,G,H,L

Russell, R.H., and Eddy, P.A., 1972, Geohydrologic evaluation of Aeneas Lake-Horse Springs Coulee, Okanogan County, Washington: Washington State Department of Ecology Technical Report 72-2, 31 p., 2 pls.   D,G,L,R

Sapik, D.B., Bortleson, G.C., Drost, B.W., Jones, M.A., and Prych, E.A., 1989, Ground-water resources and simulation of flow in aquifers containing freshwater and seawater, Island County, Washington: U.S. Geological Survey Water-Resources Investigations Report 87-4182, 4 sheets. (Available at *http://pubs.er.usgs.gov/publication/wri874182.*)   C,D,G, H,K,L, M,Q

Savoca, M.E., Johnson, K.H., and Fasser, E.T., 2009, Shallow groundwater movement in the Skagit River Delta area, Skagit County, Washington: U.S. Geological Survey Scientific Investigations Report 2009-5208, 22 p. (Available at *http://pubs.er.usgs.gov/publication/sir20095208.*)   D,G,H, L,S

Savoca, M.E., Johnson, K.H., Sumioka, S.S., Olsen, T.D., Fasser, E.T., and Huffman, R.L., 2009, Hydrogeologic framework, groundwater movement, and water budget in tributary subbasins and vicinity, lower Skagit River basin, Skagit and Snohomish Counties, Washington: U.S. Geological Survey Scientific Investigations Report 2009-5270, 46 p. (Available at *http://pubs.er.usgs.gov/publication/sir20095270.*)   B,D,G, H,L,S

Savoca, M.E., Welch, W.B., Johnson, K.H., Lane, R.C., Clothier, B.G., and Fasser, E.T., 2010, Hydrogeologic framework, groundwater movement, and water budget in the Chambers-Clover Creek Watershed and vicinity, Pierce County, Washington: U.S. Geological Survey Scientific Investigations Report 2010-5055, 46 p. (Available at *http://pubs.er.usgs.gov/publication/sir20105055.*)   B,D,G, H,L,S

Sceva, J.E., 1957, Geology and ground-water resources of Kitsap County, Washington: U.S. Geological Survey Water-Supply Paper 1413, 178 p. (Available at *http://pubs.er.usgs.gov/publication/wsp1413.*)   C,D,G, H,L,Q

Sceva, J.E., and Wegner, D.E., 1955, Records of wells and springs, water levels, and quality of ground water in central Pierce County, Washington: U.S. Geological Survey Open-File Report 55-160, 261 p. (Available at *http://pubs.er.usgs.gov/publication/ofr55160.*)   C,D,L

Simonds, F.W., 2002, Simulation of ground-water flow and potential contaminant transport at Area 6 Landfill, Naval Air Station Whidbey Island, Island County, Washington U.S. Geological Survey Water-Resources Investigations Report 01-4252, 52 p. (Available at *http://pubs.er.usgs.gov/publication/wri014252.*)   G,H,M

Simonds, F.W., and Sinclair, K.A., 2002, Surface water - ground water interactions along the lower Dungeness River and vertical hydraulic conductivity of streambed sediments, Clallam County, Washington, September 1999 - July 2001: U.S. Geological Survey Water-Resources Investigations Report 02-4161, 62 p. (Available at *http://pubs.er.usgs.gov/publication/wri024161.*)   D,G,H, K,L,S

Simonds, F.W., Longpré, C.I., and Justin, G.B., 2004, Ground-water system in the Chimacum Creek Basin and surface water/ground water interaction in Chimacum and Tarboo Creeks and the Big and Little Quilcene Rivers, Eastern Jefferson County, Washington: U.S. Geological Survey Scientific Investigations Report 2004-5058, 49 p. (Available at *http://pubs.er.usgs.gov/publication/sir20045058.*)   D,G,H, L,S

Sinclair, K.A., 2001, Assessment of surface water and groundwater interchange within the Muck Creek watershed, Pierce County: Washington State Department of Ecology Publication No. 01-03-037, 148 p. (accessed March 8, 2012, at *http://www.ecy.wa.gov/pubs/0103037.pdf*).   C,D,G, H,L,S

Sinclair, K.A., and Garrigues, R.S., 1994, Geology, water resources, and seawater intrusion assessment of Marrowstone Island, Jefferson County, Washington: Washington State Department of Ecology, Water-Supply Bulletin No. 59, 83 p. (accessed March 8, 2012, at *http://www.ecy.wa.gov/programs/eap/wsb/wsb_All.html#p59*).   C,D,G, H,L,Q

Sinclair, K.A., and Hirschey, S.J., 1992, A hydrogeologic investigation of the Scatter Creek/Black River area, southern Thurston County, Washington State: Olympia, Evergreen State College, M.S. thesis, 192 p., 8 pls.   B,C,D, G,K,L, Q,U

Stasney, D.V., 2000, Hydrostratigraphy, groundwater flow, and nitrate transport within the Abbotsford Sumas aquifer, Whatcom County, Washington: Bellingham, Western Washington University, M.S. thesis, 154 p., 1 CD-ROM disk.   C,D,G, H,K,L, M,Q

Staubitz, W.W., Bortleson, G.C., Semans, S.D., Tesoriero, A.J., and Black, R.W., 1997, Water-quality assessment of the Puget Sound Basin, Washington –Environmental setting and its implications for water quality and aquatic biota: U.S. Geological Survey Water-Resources Investigations Report 97-4013, 76 p. (Available at *http://pubs.er.usgs.gov/publication/wri974013*.)   G,Q,R, S,U

Stevens, L.G., 1991, Hydrostratigraphy and potential problems of seawater intrusion on northern Camano Island, WA: Bellingham, Western Washington University, M.S. thesis, 115 p.   C,D,G, L,Q

Sullivan, W.M., 2005, Hydrogeology of North Lummi Island, Washington: Bellingham, Western Washington University, M.S. thesis, 351 p.   B,C,D,G, H,L,Q

Sumioka, S.S., and Bauer, H.S., 2003, Estimating ground-water recharge from precipitation on Whidbey and Camano Islands, Island County, Washington, water years 1998 and 1999: U.S. Geological Survey Water-Resources Investigations Report 03-4101, 49 p. (Available at *http://pubs.er.usgs.gov/publication/wri034101*.)   B

Sumioka, S.S., and Dinicola, R.S., 2009, Groundwater/surface-water interactions in the Tunk, Bonaparte, Antoine, and Tonasket Creek subbasins, Okanogan River basin, north-central Washington, 2008: U.S. Geological Survey Scientific Investigations Report 2009-5143, 27 p. (Available at *http://pubs.er.usgs.gov/publication/sir20095143*.)   D,G,H, L,S

Thomas, B.E., Goodman, L.A., and Olsen, T.D., 1999, Hydrogeologic assessment of the Sequim-Dungeness area, Clallam County, Washington: U.S. Geological Survey Water-Resources Investigations Report 99-4048, 165 p.(Available at *http://pubs.er.usgs.gov/publication/wri994048*.)   C,D,G,H, K,L,Q

Thomas, B.E., Wilkinson, J.M., and Embrey, S.S., 1997, The ground-water system and ground-water quality in western Snohomish County, Washington: U.S. Geological Survey Water-Resources Investigations Report 96-4312, 218 p. (Available at *http://pubs.er.usgs.gov/publication/wri964312*.)   B,C,D, G,H,K, L,Q

Tooley, J., and Erickson, D., 1996, Nooksack watershed surficial aquifer characterization: Washington State Department of Ecology Publication No. 96-311, 27 p. (accessed March 8, 2012, at *http://www.ecy.wa.gov/pubs/96311.pdf*).   G,H,Q,R

28

Turney, G.L., 1986, Quality of ground water in the Puget Sound region, Washington: U.S. Geological Survey Water-Resources Investigations Report 84-4258, 170 p. (Available at *http://pubs.er.usgs.gov/publication/wri844258.*) — C,Q

Turney, G.L., Kahle, S.C., and Dion, N.P., 1995, Geohydrology and groundwater quality of east King County, Washington: U.S. Geological Survey Water-Resources Investigations Report 94-4082, 123 p. (Available at *http://pubs.er.usgs.gov/publication/wri944082.*) — B,C,D,G, H,K,L, Q,U

U.S. Geological Survey, 2009, USGS water data for Washington, 2009: U.S. Geological Survey Fact Sheet 2009-3082, 4 p. (Available at *http://pubs.er.usgs.gov/publication/fs20093082.*) — U

Vaccaro, J.J., 1992, Plan of study for the Puget-Willamette lowland Regional Aquifer System Analysis, western Washington and western Oregon: U.S. Geological Survey Water-Resources Investigations Report 91-4189, 41 p. (Available at *http://pubs.er.usgs.gov/publication/wri914189.*) — G,K

Van Denburgh, A.S., and Santos, J.F., 1965, Ground water in Washington: Its chemical and physical quality: Washington State Department of Conservation, Division of Water Resources, Water-Supply Bulletin No. 24, 93 p. (accessed March 8, 2012, at *http://www.ecy.wa.gov/programs/eap/wsb/wsb_All.html#p24*). — C,Q

van Heeswijk, Marijke, and Smith, D.T., 2002, Simulation of the ground-water flow system at Naval Submarine Base Bangor and vicinity, Kitsap County, Washington: U.S. Geological Survey Water-Resources Investigations Report 02-4261, 142 p. (Available at *http://pubs.er.usgs.gov/publication/wri024261.*) — G,H,K,M

Wallace, E.F., 1961, A preliminary report on the geology and ground-water resources of the Duck Lake area, Okanogan County, Washington: Washington State Department of Conservation, Division of Water Resources, Report No. OFTR 61-01, 20 p. (accessed March 8, 2012, at *http://www.ecy.wa.gov/pubs/oftr6101.pdf*). — G,H,R

Wallace, E.F., and Molenaar, Dee, 1961, Geology and ground-water resources of Thurston County, Washington, Vol. 1: Washington State Department of Conservation, Division of Water Resources, Water-Supply Bulletin No. 10, v. 1, 254 p. (accessed March 12, 2012, at *http://www.ecy.wa.gov/programs/eap/wsb/wsb_All.html#p10a*). — C,D,G, H,L,Q

Walters, K.L., 1971, Reconnaissance of sea-water intrusion along coastal Washington, 1966–68: Washington State Department of Ecology Water-Supply Bulletin No. 32, 208 p. (accessed March 8, 2012, at *http://www.ecy.wa.gov/programs/eap/wsb/wsb_All.html#p32*). — C,D,L,Q

Walters, K.L., 1960, Availability of ground water at the border stations at Laurier and Ferry, Washington: U.S. Geological Survey Circular 422, 12 p. (Available at *http://pubs.er.usgs.gov/publication/cir422.*) — D,G,K,L

Walters, K.L., Haushild, W.L., and Nelson, L.M., 1979, Water resources of the Lower Elwha Indian Reservation, Washington: U.S. Geological Survey Water-Resources Investigations Open-File Report 79-82, 55 p. (Available at *http://pubs.er.usgs.gov/publication/wri7982.*) — C,D,G, H,L,Q,S

Walters, K.L., and Kimmel, G.E., 1968, Ground-water occurrence and stratigraphy of unconsolidated deposits, central Pierce County, Washington: Washington State Department of Water Resources, Water-Supply Bulletin No. 22, 428 p. (accessed March 8, 2012, at *http://www.ecy.wa.gov/programs/eap/wsb/wsb_All.html#p22*). — C,D,G, H,L,Q,U

Walters, K.L., and Nassar, E.G., 1974, Water in the Methow River basin, Washington: Washington State Department of Ecology Water-Supply Bulletin No. 38, 73 p. (accessed March 8, 2012, at *http://www.ecy.wa.gov/programs/eap/wsb/wsb_All.html#p38*). — C,D,G, L,Q,S

Washburn, R.L., 1957, Ground water in the Lummi Indian Reservation, Whatcom County, Washington: U.S. Geological Survey Open-File Report 57-119, 31 p. (Available at *http://pubs.er.usgs.gov/publication/ofr57119.*) — C,D,G, L,Q

Washington State Department of Ecology, 1975, Geology and water resources of the San Juan Islands, San Juan County, Washington: Washington State Department of Ecology, Water-Supply Bulletin No. 46, 171 p. (accessed March 8, 2012, at *http://www.ecy.wa.gov/programs/eap/wsb/wsb_All.html#p46*). — C,D,G, L,Q,S

Washington State Division of Water Resources, 1960, Water resources of the Nooksack River basin and certain adjacent streams: Washington State Department of Conservation, Division of Water Resources, Water-Supply Bulletin No. 12, 187 p. (accessed March 8, 2012, at *http://www.ecy.wa.gov/programs/eap/wsb/wsb_All.html#p12*). — C,D,G, H,L,Q, S,U

Weigle, J.M., and Foxworthy, B.L., 1962, Geology and ground-water resources of west-central Lewis County, Washington: Washington State Department of Conservation, Division of Water Resources, Water-Supply Bulletin No. 17, 248 p. (accessed March 8, 2012, at *http://www.ecy.wa.gov/programs/eap/wsb/wsb_All.html#p17*). — C,D,G,H, L,Q,U

Weigle, J.M., and Mundorff, M.J., 1952, Records of wells, water levels, and quality of ground water in the Spokane Valley, Spokane County, Washington: U.S. Geological Survey State of Washington Ground-Water Report 2, 102 p. — C,D,L

Welch, W.B., and Savoca, M.E., 2011, Hydrogeologic framework of the Johns Creek subbasin and vicinity, Mason County, Washington: U.S. Geological Survey Scientific Investigations Report 2011–5168, 16 p., 1 pl. (Available at *http://pubs.er.usgs.gov/publication/sir20115168.*) — D,G,R

Whiteman, K.J., Molenaar, Dee, Jacoby, J.M., and Bortleson, G.C., 1983, Occurrence, quality, and use of ground water in Orcas, San Juan, Lopez, and Shaw Islands, San Juan County, Washington: U.S. Geological Survey Water-Resources Investigations Report 83-4019, 12 sheets. (Available at *http://pubs.er.usgs.gov/publication/wri834019.*) — C,D,G,H, L,Q,U

Wildrick, L.L., Davidson, Don, Sinclair, K.A., and Barker, Bruce, 1995, Initial watershed assessment, Water Resource Inventory Area 23, upper Chehalis River; Draft: Washington State Department of Ecology Open-File Technical Report 95-3, 67 p. — R

Woodward, D.G., Packard, F.A., Dion, N.P., and Sumioka, S.S., 1995, Occurrence and quality of groundwater in southwestern King County, Washington: U.S. Geological Survey Water-Resources Investigations Report 92-4098, 69 p. (Available at *http://pubs.er.usgs.gov/publication/wri924098.*) — B,C,D, G,H,L, Q

Wozniewicz, J.V., 1989, Hydrogeology of the Chamokane valley aquifer system: Cheney, Eastern Washington University, M.S. thesis, 172 p. — D,G,H, K,L,M

Wyman, S.A., 1993, The potential for heavy metal migration from sediments of Coeur d'Alene Lake into the Rathdrum Prairie aquifer, Kootenai County, Idaho: Moscow, University of Idaho, M.S. thesis, 141 p. — C,D,G, K,L,Q,S

Zheng, Yi, 1995, Distribution of major and trace metals in groundwater of the Spokane   C,D,G,
  aquifer, northeastern Washington–Water quality and river/aquifer interaction: Cheney,   L,Q
  Eastern Washington University, M.S. thesis, 123 p. (Abstract accessed March 8, 2012,
  at *http://www.geology.ewu.edu/dept/zheng.htm.*)

Acknowledgments

Lee Walkling, Librarian for Washington's Division of Geology and Earth Resources, provided much assistance in locating documents for the authors' review. Lori Tuck, Hydrologist in the USGS Montana Water Science Center, provided loan copies of many documents that were otherwise unavailable. USGS Libraries in Menlo Park, California and Denver, Colorado promptly provided loan copies of additional documents needed for review. James R. Bartolino (Groundwater Specialist in the USGS Idaho Water Science Center) and Bob Bergantino (Montana Bureau of Mines and Geology, retired) provided peer reviews of the document that resulted in the addition of key documents relating to groundwater in Idaho and Montana, respectively.

References Cited

Briar, D.W., Lawlor, S.M., Stone, M.A.J., Parliman, D.J., Schaefer, J.L., and Kendy, Eloise, 1996, Ground-water levels in the intermontane basins of the northern Rocky Mountains, Montana and Idaho: U.S. Geological Survey Hydrologic Investigations Atlas HA-738-B, 1 sheet, scale 1:750,000. (Available at *http://pubs.er.usgs.gov/publication/ha738B.*)

Clark, D.W., and Dutton, D.M., 1996, Quality of ground water and surface water in intermontane basins of the northern Rocky Mountains, Montana and Idaho: U.S. Geological Survey Hydrologic Investigations Atlas HA-738-C, 1 sheet, scale 1:750,000. (Available at *http://pubs.er.usgs.gov/publication/ha738C.*

Jones, M.A., 1990, Selected references for the Puget–Willamette lowland Regional Aquifer System study, Puget Sound lowland, Washington: U.S. Geological Survey Open-File Report 90-584, 55 p. (Available at *http://pubs.er.usgs.gov/publication/ofr90584.*)

MacInnis, J.D., Lackaff, B.B., Buchanan, J.P., Boese, R.M., McHugh, J., Harvey, G., Higdem, R., and Stevens, G., 2009, The Spokane Valley-Rathdrum Prairie aquifer atlas 2009 update: Spokane, Spokane Aquifer Joint Board, 26 p. (accessed March 8, 2012, at *http://www.spokanecounty.org/loaddoc.aspx?docid=4487.*)

Tuck, L.K., Briar, D.W., and Clark, D.W., 1996, Geologic history and hydrogeologic units of intermontane basins of the northern Rocky Mountains, Montana and Idaho: U.S. Geological Survey Hydrologic Investigations Atlas HA-738-A, scale 1:750,000, sheet 1. (Available at *http://pubs.er.usgs.gov/publication/ha738A.*)

Whitehead, R.L., 1994, Ground-water atlas of the United States, segment 7, Idaho, Oregon, and Washington: U.S. Geological Survey Hydrologic Investigations Atlas HA-730-H, 31 p. (Available at *http://pubs.er.usgs.gov/publication/ha730H.*)

Whitehead, R.L., 1996, Ground-water atlas of the United States, segment 8, Montana, North Dakota, South Dakota, and Wyoming: U.S. Geological Survey Hydrologic Investigations Atlas HA-730-I, 24 p. (Available at *http://pubs.er.usgs.gov/publication/ha730I.*)

Wiltshire, D.A., Lyford, F.P., and Cohen, A.J., 1986, Bibliography on ground water in glacial-aquifer systems in the Northeastern United States: U.S. Geological Survey Circular 972, 26 p. (Available at *http://pubs.er.usgs.gov/publication/cir972.*)